THE LAW THAT SETS YOU FREE!

Book of James

Discovery Books

THE LAW THAT SETS YOU FREE!

DAVID H. ROPER

Book of James

Word Books, Publisher
Waco, Texas

DISCOVERY BOOKS are published by Word Books Publishers,
in cooperation with Discovery Foundation,
Palo Alto, California.

ISBN 0-8499-0003-4
Library of Congress catalog card number: 77-075455
Printed in the United States of America

For

Randy
Brian
and
Joshua

Plants that are growing up (Ps. 144:12).

Contents

Preface

Most people feel that the Book of James is nothing more than a string of unconnected maxims without an obvious theme or thread—a sort of homily of practical advice and counsel. The intriguing thing about this work, however, is that it really is a unified whole. Once the connecting framework comes to light, it falls into place in a satisfying and harmonious way. What appear at first to be various scattered thoughts on a random series of subjects turns out to be connected teachings, all set against a common backdrop with which we can easily identify. That backdrop is suffering.

"Oh no," you groan. "I don't want to hear about suffering. I thought the Christian message was one of hope and joy. Why is there such a need to focus on suffering?"

Well, the point of James' letter is *not* suffering, itself. Rather James is addressing himself to certain common, natural responses people make to suffering and pressure. When we come to the end of his letter, we have a completely uncommon view of (1) how to respond to suffering and oppression and affliction, and (2) how to counsel others in similar situations. It is different from the world's view because it is based on faith—authentic, saving faith—which might also be seen as another central teaching of James' book.

What do we—most of us, anyway—naturally do in the

face of some kind of pressure? It doesn't have to be anything worse than a nighttime drip in the bathroom sink.
Or it can be in the form of unasked for (and probably
undeserved) criticism by a so-called friend—all the way to
truly trying circumstances that go beyond natural understanding or endurance. Our responses range through the
following: blame someone else, get on the good side of
someone, rationalize, raid the refrigerator, or—and this is
subtle—blame God. Furthermore, how do we, generally
speaking, tend to counsel people in trouble? "Hang in
there!" "You *poor* thing!" "How *dare* he say such a thing!"
And so on.

But James will have no part of any of that. What we
discover (and this is not particularly comfortable to hear)
is that our natural responses are usually *sinful,* or at the
very least, totally unhelpful. Therefore, counsel along lines
that support those responses is actually leading people into
sin, or at the least, wasting their precious time.

James exhorts, counsels, urges: see your troubles from
God's perspective, and don't use them as an excuse to do
wrong. The outcome of such a changed, supernatural attitude is a visible, viable, saving faith which is growing
strong because it consistently takes hold of God and allows
him to use the pressures to our certain benefit, as well as
to the wonder of people around us, and definitely to his
own glory.

1

Suffering Successfully

James 1:1–4

I recall someone once saying that every time he read the Book of James, he got the uneasy feeling that James had been reading his mail. I always feel like he's been reading my mind! Like most Christians I have a lot of sins that I want to keep under cover. But James won't allow that. He deals in ruthless exposure.

The Book of James calls us to transparency and honesty. As far as James is concerned, honesty is not the best policy—it is the only policy. This book, is essentially a cry of outrage against hypocrisy in all its forms. He speaks out against the great social sins of his day and ours—racism, oppression of minorities, and warmongering, but he doesn't stop there. He bears down on the secret inner sins of pride and jealousy and defensiveness, and unleashes his big guns there—54 commands in 108 verses. As someone has said, James doesn't merely strafe the deck, he drops the bomb right down the funnel. To James, God's Word is the "royal law," the rule of the King, and, therefore, calls for instantaneous, unquestioning obedience at the deepest level of our experience.

Here is James' brief salutation: "James, a servant of God and of the Lord Jesus Christ, To the twelve tribes in the Dispersion: Greeting" (James 1:1, RSV).

There is nothing special about this greeting from a literary standpoint. Letters in the ancient world normally opened with the name of the writer, followed by the name of the recipient, or recipients, and a word of greeting. James follows this time-honored precedent in his letter, as do almost all the writers of New Testament letters—a fact that always impresses me again with God's "down-to-earth" quality and the earthiness of God's book. If that term offends you, I want you to understand that it is merely my way of stressing God's passion for communication. When God speaks, he does so not through technical jargon but through the common things of life. Plain talk through plain people—that is God's way. The language and style of the New Testament are not in general that of the classical literature of that time, but it is the language of the common people—the bold, idiomatic street-talk of the day. It is good to keep that fact in mind as we read God's Word and as we attempt to translate that message by life and word into our culture. That way we will maintain the same relevancy in our society that these letters had in their original setting.

Now a word about this brief introduction: First the author introduces himself. The name of the writer is given simply as James, as if no further identification is necessary. Evidently, it was not for the original readers, but it does pose a problem for us. There are three New Testament characters who bore that name (not including the James of Luke 6:16)—there were the two apostles, "James the less" (i.e., "the little one") and James the son of Zebedee, who are well known to us since they belonged to the apostolic band. But we are quite certain that neither of these men wrote this book. There are compelling reasons which we won't go into here, but which you may want to pursue on your own. There is a third, "James the Lord's brother" who is almost universally recognized as the writer of this letter. He appears in Mark 6:3 as one of the four brothers of Jesus—the others being Joses, Judas (or Jude), and Simon (of whom we know virtually nothing). They may have been children of Joseph and Mary born after Jesus' birth, or they may have been Joseph's children by a prior marriage. We simply don't know. The details of this controversy, however, are unimportant. The crucial issue is that the author of the book is almost certainly our Lord's brother, or to be more exact, his step-brother or half-brother since Jesus, being born of God and not Joseph, would not have been genetically related to Joseph under any set of circumstances. It does appear, however, that all four sons were raised together in Joseph's home and thus shared the same environment in their most formative years.

A PERFECT BROTHER

According to Mark (and to a lesser degree, according to Matthew and Luke), the brothers, to put it mildly, lacked understanding of Jesus and his ministry. And could they be blamed? Jesus, I'm sure, was an exceptional child. Though he developed in a normal way, as we are told, he was (and here, admittedly, I am speculating) probably precocious—a bright, healthy, attractive young man with great social appeal. Furthermore, we know that he did not sin—a fact that would be discouraging to younger brothers, to say the least, and at times downright annoying. Have you ever had a *perfect* older brother? If you have, I'm sure you would understand. Even in my home, with no impeccable children (or parents), I occasionally hear one of my younger sons say, "But Randy [the oldest] *never* gets disciplined." Of course he does (even if he is 6'1"), but I'm certain the scales do seem imbalanced at times. And how much more difficult it must have been for Jesus' younger brothers. Wouldn't it be bothersome to have an older brother who always obeyed—promptly, cheerfully, and without argument? Jesus evidently always did. And, furthermore, having been told what Joseph and Mary desired and assuming that it was not contrary to his heavenly Father's desires, I believe he *always* fulfilled those expectations. Which must mean that even as a small child he always picked up his toys and put them away, always washed the ring out of the washtub, faithfully did his chores without being reminded, etc. He was a model child. Furthermore, Mary could have been excused for being a bit partial to him since she knew of his unique conception and destiny. Evidently his brothers did not.

Is it any wonder that his brothers resented him? I fear I would do no better. We are told that at one point his brothers set out to seize him, thinking that he had lost his mind (Mark 3:20–21). Then in Mark 6:1–6 on the occasion of his rejection at Nazareth Jesus declares that a prophet is not without honor except in his own hometown and among his own relatives and in his own household. And here, so there can be no question as to who those relatives are, they are listed by Mark, and all the brothers are named. This lack of regard is further underscored in John 7:3–8 where the apostle flatly declares that Jesus' brothers did not believe in him. Perhaps it is not reading too much into John 19:26–27 to see there the attitude of the brothers toward Jesus even as they stood at the foot of the cross when Jesus committed his mother to John the Apostle as her "son." I believe, therefore, that Jesus' brothers were, throughout most of his earthly life, actively hostile toward him and his ministry.

But the resurrection radically changed them. The Apostle Paul records in 1 Corinthians 15 with brevity and poignancy that after the resurrection Jesus appeared to Peter and to the 500 and then to his brother James. That was almost certainly the turning point for this brother, as well as the rest of the family. The "brothers of the Lord" appear conspicuously in the early church (Acts 1:14; 1 Cor. 9:5); Jude wrote the little epistle in the New Testament that bears his name, and James became a pillar of the church along with Peter and John (Gal. 2:9). The fact that James's name usually occurs first alongside theirs suggests the high regard with which he was held. In Acts 12:17 the church in Jerusalem is described as "James and the brethren," an indication of his status there. In Acts 21:18 he once more appears with the Jerusalem church and its elders. Except for the opening verse of this letter, the only other mention of James in the New Testament is in Jude 1, where the fact that Jude is the "brother of James" is considered sufficient to authenticate his authority as the writer.

JAMES THE JUST

There are, in addition, some very significant statements about James outside the New Testament. Josephus (*Antiquities* XX. 9, 1) states that James was martyred for his belief by order of the high priest Annas II. A second-century Christian writer, Hegesippus, whose writings were preserved in the *Church History* of Eusebius (II. 23), tells us further that James was widely known for his conspicuous devotion. He writes,

> James, the brother of our Lord, as there were many of his name was surnamed "the Just" by all from the days of our Lord until now. He received the government of the church with the apostles. He drank neither wine nor strong drink and abstained from animal food and a razor never came upon his head. He never wore woolen but only fine linen garments. He was in the habit of entering into the temple alone and was often found upon his bended knees asking for the forgiveness

of the people so that his knees became hard like a camel's knees as the consequence of his habitual supplication and kneeling before God.

Hegesippus further tells us that James was martyred in Jerusalem. His body was hurled from the pinnacle of the temple and battered beyond recognition by a priest wielding a fuller's club. One indication of the strength of a man's conviction is whether or not he is willing to die for it. James died because he believed that Jesus was the Son of God. He was martyred after the outbreak of the Jewish war against Rome (A.D. 66–67). The ancient Christian writers were convinced that the murder of James sealed the fate of the city of Jerusalem, which fell to the Romans in A.D. 70. This, then, is something of the life and character of the author of this book whom the early church rightly called "James the Just."

Note, however, how he designates himself in the introduction, "James, a bondservant of God and of the Lord Jesus Christ," not "James, the brother of Christ." He passes an opportunity for cosmic name-dropping. He does so because, like the Apostle Paul, he no longer knows Jesus after the flesh (2 Cor. 5:16). The former relationship is irrelevant. Now Jesus is Lord. He describes himself here as both a servant of God—a common phrase in the Old Testament for anyone dedicated to God's service—and a servant of the Lord Jesus Christ, the usual designation of Christians. The combination of both Old Testament and New Testament titles here is unique in the New Testament. Perhaps it suggests James' new frame of reference: the Jesus he knew as a boy was surely Emmanuel, "God with us," Yahweh of Israel become flesh. Thus, James is no longer brother, but bondservant—of God and the Lord Jesus Christ—both one, since no man can serve two masters.

Now a word about the recipients of this letter—"the twelve tribes in the Dispersion." The mention of the twelve tribes immediately calls to mind the twelve tribes of Israel. The question to be answered, however, is whether James has in mind Jewish Christians alone or is thinking metaphorically of spiritual Israel, i.e., the entire Christian community, Jew and Gentile, dispersed throughout the Roman Empire. Unfortunately, we may never know the complete answer to that question until we meet the author. I do, however, have some thoughts.

The book has a decidedly "Jewish" flavor. The terminology and illustrations are drawn from the Old Testament; the idioms and literary style are Hebraic or Aramaic. The entire book actually reads like one of the Old Testament prophets and could, by the omission of only a few words in the introduction (i.e., "Lord Jesus Christ," 1:1), fit nicely into the Old Testament collection. (The term *church* in 5:14 can also have the meaning of assembly or congregation and even in the New Testament is used of Israel—see Acts 7:38; Heb. 2:12.) In fact, so "Jewish" is this book that some writers have conjectured that it was a Hebrew work adapted for use in the early church by the addition of the distinctively Christian introduction. I disagree, however. It seems best to read this book as it has traditionally been received—as a letter written to the Jewish-Christian community very early in the church's history before the Apostle Paul's great missionary thrust into the gentile world. It appears that the book is quite early, probably written before the council in Jerusalem in A.D. 50 (Acts 15). They were still meeting in synagogues (see 2:2 where "assembly" translates the Greek word *synagogue*), and therefore were in an early period in the church's history when Christians were still considered a sect within Judaism.

OLD CONCEPTS INTO LIVING PRINCIPLES

The recipients were Christians to be sure, but steeped in Jewish tradition and lore and rooted in the Old Testament in their thinking. It is probable that no other New Testament book had been written yet. James leads off, so to speak, in an attempt to translate Old Testament concepts into living principles in the church. At least it is good to keep that concept in mind as you try to understand and interpret the book. You have to think like a Jew who has no knowledge of the New Testament, which was not yet written: who is attempting to relate his ancient and time-honored faith to the new idea that the covenant God of Israel had become flesh and dwelt among his people and was now the ascended Lord and Messiah. A staggering concept to say the least, and one that would be difficult to assimilate into one's catalogue of beliefs. James, or at least so I believe, was the first New Testament writer to tackle that assignment.

In referring to these Jewish Christians, James describes them as those who are *dispersed abroad.* The term *diaspora* meaning "sown abroad" is normally used of Jews scattered throughout the ancient world as a result of repeated persecutions. It is odd, therefore, that James uses this term for Jewish *Christians* unless he is thinking symbolically of these believing Jews as though they were in a dispersion similar to Israel's. And so I believe they were. This was a suffering community. The letter so indicates. I believe these Jews, because they had embraced Jesus as the Messiah, were being hounded and harassed by the Jewish community. Driven from their homes, schools and shops, they were a diaspora within a diaspora. As Jews they had been driven from their homeland. As Christians they were being driven from their Jewish communities. These were businessmen whose shops were being boycotted, laborers whose wages were being fraudulently withheld, professionals whose services were never used. Children were being driven from homes, scholars from their tenured positions in schools. Rejected by their Jewish brethren and despised by the gentile community they were men without a country, a Diaspora.

A WORD OF GREETING

To those hounded and hated people James addresses a brief salutation: "Greeting." But that translation really doesn't do justice to the meaning of the original term. Its actual meaning is "be joyful" or "be of good cheer." Or as we might say it, "cheer up!" It is the term that appears repeatedly in the Book of Philippians and is translated "rejoice" (Phil. 1:18; 2:17, 18, 28; 3:1; 4:10). That is indeed an unusual greeting to people in such depressing circumstances. But that quite honestly is always God's word to us in times of crisis and pressure—cheer up, the best is yet to be. I once heard a friend respond with the reply to a question about his state of being that he was "doing okay under the circumstances," to which the inquirer said, "Under the circumstances? What are you doing under there?" Good words, I think. God has something better for us than being under the pile. God's children, of all people, ought to be optimistic, positive, cheerful people. After all, Jesus said "Be of good cheer; I have overcome the world." Therefore, why all the gloom?

We have to take seriously the fact that the readers of this letter are *commanded* to buck up. This is not merely good advice. Pessimism and despair, if persisted in, become acts of disobedience. The writers of Scripture, however, unlike most of our attempts to cheer up another, never engage in platitudes. There is compelling content behind every ad-

monition. They supply both reasons and resources for
obedience and these James spells out in the opening paragraph of his letter:

> Consider it all joy, my brethren, when you encounter various
> trials, knowing that the testing of your faith produces endur-
> ance. And let endurance have its perfect result, that you may
> be perfect and complete, lacking in nothing (James 1:2–4).

I have spent a considerable amount of time talking to
people about the matter of suffering. The question is usually posed this way, "Why do the innocent suffer?" My
answer is always the same: "I don't know." To be sure, I
do know the classic theological answers to that question,
but they never really satisfy me or anyone else I find. At
least they don't satisfy my heart. At the present what *does*
give me rest is to leave the matter where Job does—in the
hands of a sovereign, wise Lord of the universe—and allow
God to be God, knowing that the judge of all the world will
do what is right. I don't think I have any other answer yet
to that age-old conundrum. However, while I do not yet
know precisely *why* the righteous suffer, I do know *how*
they should suffer—and it is this question that James takes
up in verses 2 through 4. In this section James tells us *how
to suffer successfully.*

CALL TO REJOICE

James begins with a command: *"Consider it joy* when you
encounter various trials." The closing word of verse 1
translated *cheer up* or *rejoice* is taken up by *joy* in verse 2.
The connection can't really be reproduced in English except by some paraphrase such as "Greet trials cheerfully."
Unusual counsel to put it mildly.

Furthermore, James tells us, such suffering is *inevitable.*
He does not say "consider it all joy *if* you meet various
trials." He says *when.* Suffering is not an elective. It is a

required course. You can count on it. Peter states a kindred truth when he writes,

> Beloved, do not be surprised at the fiery ordeal which comes upon you to prove you, as though something strange were happening to you. But rejoice in so far as you share Christ's sufferings, that you may also rejoice and be glad when his glory is revealed (1 Pet. 4:12, 13, RSV).

Suffering ought never to strike us as a strange thing. In fact, we ought to feel right at home with it. Or as Paul emphatically states the principle, "For to you it has been granted for Christ's sake, not only to believe in Him, but also to suffer for His sake" (Phil. 1:29). Both faith and suffering are gifts of grace (for so the verb "granted" implies). We deserve neither, but we get both. For believers, suffering is clearly the name of the game. Now this is not to say that the Christian life is one interminable grind; not at all. This certainly has not been my experience at least. However, we need to know that we will "encounter" (James 1:2) trials along the way, and we should not be surprised by that encounter. There is, by the way, a very interesting use of this word *encounter* in the story of the man on the road to Jericho who "fell among" thieves (Luke 10:25–37). (The verb translated "fell among" in Luke 10:30 is the same word as the one translated "encounter" in James 1:2. These robbers are said to have beaten him, stripped him and left him for dead (an apt description I think of our feelings when assailed by trials!). And like the man on the way to Jerico, we also "encounter" trials along the way. Such trials are not a continuous experience in our journey but are nevertheless to be expected intermittently along the way. Suffering, James declares, is inevitable. We should not be shocked or surprised. Rather we should greet such onslaughts cheerfully.

Are you now engaged in some titanic struggle, passing through anxious days and sleepless nights? Does it comfort you to be told to greet such an encounter cheerfully? I suspect it does not. I'm frequently reminded of the man who was told to "cheer up, things could be worse." And the next day, sure enough, they were worse. Who needs that kind of help? I can't merely give my emotions a good shake and snap out of it (whatever "it" is). And, of course, that is not what James is saying. This is not some vapid exhortation to smile and fake it or look on the brighter side of things. Indeed it is not! It is rather a call to rejoice based on the knowledge of certain well-attested facts. The key word is *knowing*. Only when you know certain truths can you properly respond to suffering. James follows, then, with a statement of the basic truth that will enable one to enjoy rather than endure his circumstances.

The fundamental fact that James wants his readers to know is that suffering is purposeful! "The testing of your faith *produces* steadfastness." In other words, pain is productive. The problem with so much of our suffering is that we do not seem to be going anywhere. We feel as though God has put us on a siding and left us sitting idle while life passes us by. But that is not true. Rightly utilized suffering produces an eternally valuable commodity.

TUNNEL TIMES

I remember once reading a paper entitled "Advice While in the Tunnel." The writer, whose name I've since forgotten, pointed out that frequently we undergo periods of darkness when all the light goes out of our life. Those periods he described as time spent in a tunnel. Now, he said, there are several things to remember when in a tunnel. The first is that tunnels are always on the main route, never on a siding. Second, tunnels are a necessary part of the journey because that is the only way to get through the

mountains to one's destination. Therefore, we need to view
these dark periods as opportunities for progress. The worst
thing to do in a tunnel is to quit. The only way to get
through the experience is to keep moving ahead knowing
that in time you will burst out into the light and find
yourself further down the road. Now I believe that is what
James is saying. Periods of intense stress, disappointment
or grief are not indications that God has given up on us.
To the contrary, they are signs that God is at work. Or as
Paul puts it, "Momentary, light affliction is producing for
us an eternal weight of glory" (2 Cor. 4:17). Do you see the
process? Suffering works for us, not against us. It is a process that renews us. It is to be utilized for good. Suffering
is not counterproductive, but useful and purposeful.

The specific product of suffering is *endurance*. The term
suggests the capacity to remain under pressure without
collapsing. It signifies stability or staying power. That is
an admirable quality—a mark of true manhood and wom-
anhood. And unfortunately a trait hard to come by at all
times in history. Durable, tenacious men have always been
in short supply (Prov. 20:6). They are produced only by
suffering. Have you ever prayed, "Lord make me a strong
stable person"? Sure you have. I long for stability in my
life. I fancy myself planted in the soil like a thousand-year-
old oak—unshaken and unshakable, unflappable, resolute.
Or to use another analogy, I often think of Vince Lombar-
di's plaque in the Packers' dressing room: "When the going
gets tough, the tough get going." I want to be spiritually
tough. Do you know how you get tough? It comes through
suffering. There is no other way.

The process, I believe, works in this manner. There are
always areas in our lives where we are counting on ourselves and not God. We may feel adequate in ourselves, and
therefore, proud, or inadequate and, therefore, intimi-
dated. But no matter if we are self-reliant in any portion

of our life, if we believe it all depends on us, we are counting on the flesh. And since God for our sake hates the flesh and will not tolerate it in any form, he will move to bring pressure to bear on that area of our life. The purpose of that pressure is to get us to relinquish our control and allow Christ to exert his authority there—in short, to encourage us to trust him instead of ourselves, as the diagram illustrates.

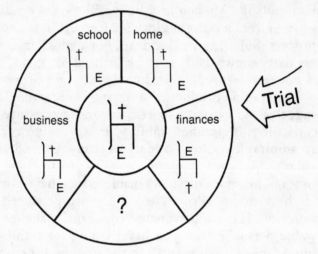

†=Christ
ʰ=Throne or seat of control
E=Ego or self

When we trust him we tap into his infinite resources and discover that everything we need is available to us—his power, his strength, his poise and stability. And therefore, we can endure. Now I don't mean to imply that the transformation is immediate or permanent, because we may again struggle in the same area. However, when we lay hold of Christ's life and resources we *can endure* for the moment, and as we gain experience we more readily resort to the Lord and thus more consistently demonstrate a stable character. It is a process, of course, that takes time, but the *product* is certain.

Do you think of yourself as basically a loving, giving person? Do you know what will happen? God will, in time, bring into your life the most difficult, irrascible, obnoxious person you ever met and set that individual squarely across your path so you cannot avoid contact with him or her. You may discover how utterly impossible he is to love and all your natural love and kindness will desert you. You'll find yourself thinking and saying things about that individual that will horrify you. Do you know what God is doing? He has his finger on an area of your life where you are not operating out of faith. It is your love you are counting on. He has to "prove" or "test" that faith—i.e., smelt or refine your faith in order to purify it—so you will stop believing in yourself and the adequacy of your love and start thinking and acting out of his love. And when you do, you have all the power in the universe to serve and care for your difficult friend.

Someone has said that God wants to squeeze us like grapes to make sweet wine. The pressures we experience are the fingers of God to effect that purpose. Suffering therefore is productive.

Now a further word of exhortation: "And let endurance have its perfect result, that you may be perfect and complete, lacking in nothing" (James 1:4). There's the rub. We do not allow the fingers of God to squeeze us. We do not let endurance go on to produce its perfect or final work. We stop short somewhere along the line and fight back. We give way to bitterness and resentment and curse God and his beneficial plan for us. We don't allow suffering to complete its work. We shout "why me?" or "it isn't fair" and miss the beauty of God's plan—and at what loss to the fulfillment of God's plan for us. James writes that God's plan is to make us perfect and complete, mature and adequate, *lacking nothing*, fully equipped for life. That's God's design and desire. Our part is to allow him the freedom to implement it. Are God's fingers pressing you today?

2

Suffering Unsuccessfully

James 1:5–27

In James 1:2–4 we are told how to suffer successfully. We are given a new perspective on suffering that will enable us to be transformed by the struggles of life rather than traumatized by them. God's plan is to make us mature and complete, and suffering is a necessary and, therefore, inevitable part of that process.

However, there are attitudes and reactions to trial that hinder God's constructive processes, and it is these hindrances that James takes up in the remaining verses of chapter 1.

But if any of you lacks wisdom, let him ask of God, who gives to all men generously and without reproach, and it will be given to him. But let him ask in faith without any doubting, for the one who doubts is like the surf of the sea driven and tossed by the wind. For let not that man expect that he will receive anything from the Lord, being a double-minded man, unstable in all his ways (James 1:5–8).

THE NEED FOR WISDOM

There are numerous passages in the Scriptures that
promise that God is our all-sufficient counsel, who gives
wisdom in times of perplexity and indecision. However,
I do not believe that is the primary meaning of this verse
in this setting. First note the context. The paragraph 1:5–8
is bracketed by the discussion on suffering. I, for my part,
believe the entire first chapter of James deals with the issue
of suffering. Therefore we must in some way relate 1:5–8
to its contextual setting.

Second, James, with his thoroughly Jewish way of looking at things, is, I believe, using the term *wisdom* in an Old
Testament sense rather than our contemporary understanding of the term. We think of wisdom today in terms
of discernment or understanding. In the Old Testament,
wisdom is almost always the practical application of knowledge rather than a theoretical comprehension of it. Wisdom
in the Old Testament sense is truth acted upon. In other
words, wisdom has to do with righteous behavior. The wise
man possessed the ability to act righteously in any circumstance. He was skilled at living life as it was intended to
be lived. A careful reading of any one of the examples of
the wisdom literature of the Old Testament such as Proverbs will establish this definition for you.

Furthermore, I believe James is using the term in its Old
Testament sense because that is the way he defines the term
in James 3:13–18. The wisdom from above (in contrast to
so-called earthly wisdom) is pure, peaceable, gentle, reasonable, full of mercy and good fruits, unwavering, without
hypocrisy. In other words the truly wise man is morally
pure, peaceful, gentle, teachable, etc. Wisdom has to do
with what he *is*, not what he knows. I should add that the
contrasting term *fool* in the Old Testament sense is not one
who knows nothing, but one who behaves badly. Nabal,

whose name means "fool," is a good illustration (1 Sam. 25).

Therefore, in James 1:3–8 the wisdom described is not the capacity merely to discern the right course of action but the actual behavior of one undergoing trials. James' concern is with those aspects of Christian character which we ought to display under pressure. Endurance is not a passive reaction. The Christian response to pain is not merely to clench our fists and set our jaws. Not at all. Far more is required. Wisdom is called for—purity, peacefulness, a nondefensive, restful spirit, a quiet joy—the character of God himself. Do you lack those qualities of wisdom? James says ask God and he gives. It is God's intention that you lack nothing (v. 4). Therefore, when you do lack peace or poise or any aspect of righteous character while suffering, ask God whom James describes literally as the "giver and not the reproacher." That is, he gives with no strings attached and he never rebukes us when we ask again and again.

If you are like me, trials make you cross and crabby and hard to live with. Whose fault is that? Only ours! We don't have to be irritable and temperamental. We can ask and receive. His resources are available upon request.

ABANDONED TO HIS WILL

But there is one proviso: we must ask in faith. Now understand how James defines faith. We will see this clearly in his second chapter, but at this point let me simply state that for James, faith involves an utter abandonment to the will of God. James is not saying that we have to somehow convince ourselves beyond any doubt that God is faithful before he will respond to us. Some people are simply incapable at their particular stage of Christian growth of conjuring up that kind of belief. Even the disciples after three and a half years of vital contact with the Lord had problems with doubt (Matt. 28:17). What it does mean is that despite our misgivings and apprehensions, we are resolutely committed to finding and doing God's will. That interpretation of James' meaning also seems certain because of the qualifying phrase "without any doubting." The term *doubting* means "to be divided in one's mind" or "to be at variance within." The antonym is to be a single-minded, undistracted or wholehearted man. He further describes the man who doubts as a double-minded (or two-souled) man. That man receives nothing from God. James is saying that God gives himself only to those who want it all. You can't enjoy God unless you are abandoned to him; you can only endure him. Like Augustine we pray, "Lord, make me pure—but not now." When we do so we tie God's hands; and we have no resources for complying with the incredible demands of the Christian life.

Do you understand what James is saying? God will give to the man who is whole-heartedly sold out to God's will, whose eye is single. In other words, God gives only to those who want *whatever* he gives. Are you content to submit to a difficult relationship if God so wills? To remain single or apparently sidelined? If so, God will give you grace equal to the demand.

Have you ever read what the writer of Hebrews said about Jesus in his most agonizing period of suffering (Heb. 5:7)? He offered up both prayers and supplications with loud crying and tears to him who was able to save him from death: "Father, if Thou art willing, remove this cup from Me; yet not My will, but Thine be done" (Luke 22:42). And, it says, he was *heard*. It was not God's will to pass the cup to someone else. He had to drink it. Therefore, to hear does not mean to spare him the anguish of the cross. He had to suffer. No one else in all the universe could take the cup. The Father so willed it and the Son submitted to that will. And because he was willing, God heard him and sustained him in his moment of trial. Do you lack staying power? Ask and it will be given.

FLOWERING GRASS

There is a second hindrance to successful suffering found in verses 9 through 12. James writes,

> But let the brother of humble circumstances glory in his high position; and let the rich man glory in his humiliation, because like flowering grass he will pass away. For the sun rises with a scorching wind, and withers the grass; and its flower falls off, and the beauty of its appearance is destroyed; so too the rich man in the midst of his pursuits will fade away (James 1:9–11).

Many of the people who would read this letter had lost everything. They had been cruelly driven from home and hearth. They had been ostracized and blackballed. I once had a friend from an orthodox Jewish home whose family, on his conversion to faith in Christ, bought a casket and symbolically buried him, never to recognize his presence again. This was the experience of those believers. Yet James writes these words: "Boast in the fact that you have been humiliated. If your possessions have been taken from you, rejoice."

These people may have been sold the humanistic philosophy that one's happiness consists in an abundance of things: if one has the right house, or clothes, or profession, or stereo, or cuff links, then he is truly alive. But that philosophy is errant, worldly nonsense. It reminds me of the comment made by a mourner at the graveside of a wealthy eccentric who was buried in his gold Cadillac, "Man, that is really living!"

"The wealthy man," James says, "fades away." And how true that is. Things do not make us happy. God makes us happy. Happiness is a by-product of belief. True satisfaction comes from God. These believers could have lost anything, and they could still rejoice, because they had everything, just as Paul describes himself as "having noth-

ing yet possessing *all things*" (2 Cor. 6:10). They were emi-
nently wealthy—heirs of all things. That is a perspective
that would establish a proper set of priorities.

Some years ago, my wife and I were watching a television report on the aftermath of an earthquake in Southern
California. The interviewer spoke to a woman standing
near the rubble that had once been her home, and as he
questioned her she began to weep. She said, "Everything
my husband and I have lived for for twenty seven years was
in that house." We couldn't help but feel compassion for
her. Nevertheless, Carolyn and I agreed that there is not
one item in our house worth living for. It will surely fade
away in time. And that is James' perspective. If God
reduces you to nothing, rejoice! You have everything. Your
true source of joy will never be taken away.

In contrast to the rich man who fades away, James describes the man who perseveres under trial: "Blessed is a
man who perseveres under trial; for once he has been approved, he will receive the crown of life, which the Lord
has promised to those who love Him" (James 1:12).

"The man who perseveres," he says, "will be approved
of God." This word *approved* is the Greek word *dokimos*
which frequently appears on pottery unearthed in the
Near East. It is the counterpart of our Good Housekeeping
seal of approval or the Underwriters' Laboratory seal. It
was placed on pottery which passed through the furnace
intact. But if the pot cracked in the firing it would be
inscribed *adokimos,* "disapproved," and perhaps go on the
budget shelf. It is this figure that James apparently has in
mind. If we endure through suffering, we gain God's Good
Housekeeping seal of approval. We have been tested and
approved dependable and trustworthy. We are not likely
to blow out or blow up under pressure.

The result, James says, is that we are blessed (happy), and
we receive the crown of life which the Lord has promised

to those who love him. I do not believe this crown is merely a future reward. It is an honor conferred upon us in this life. It is basically a state of being—a condition of life that ought to characterize every believer. The concept of a crown of life is analogous to Paul's statement about reigning in life (Rom. 5:17). It is God's intent that we live in the midst of pressure and stress as victors rather than victims. There never should be any circumstance which overwhelms us because we have an infinite adequate Lord. When we grasp that concept then we truly begin to reign over our environment like earthly kings over theirs. Is that not the force of Paul's statement in 2 Timothy 2:12, "If we endure, we shall also reign with him"?

TEST OR TEMPTATION

There is a third hindrance to rejoicing in suffering: "Let no one say when he is tempted, 'I am being tempted by God'; for God cannot be tempted by evil, and He Himself does not tempt any one" (James 1:13).

Do you blame God for your evil circumstances and consequent failures? Many people do. When suffering and sin come we are inclined to attribute the collapse to God. But James says we cannot blame God for failure in our lives. God is never the author of sin. God may test people with a view to approval; he never tempts people to sin. He is not that kind of Lord.

Now, we do need to distinguish between a test and a temptation, because the Scripture makes that distinction. A test is an experience which *God* brings into our life in order to build us. A temptation comes from *Satan*. It is designed to cause us to sin. But the amazing thing is that *any* circumstance can be either a test or a temptation, depending upon our response to it.

Let me illustrate this principle from the Book of Job, the opening chapters of which are a dialogue between Satan and the Lord. Satan points to the Lord's servant Job and suggests that Job's faithfulness is actually based on his prosperity. "But," he says, "allow me to touch his body, or his family, or his possessions, and he will curse you." And so God granted permission to Satan to rain blows on Job and his family. Job lost it all. He lost his wealth, his flocks and herds, his home, and his sons and daughters. Then Satan, having reported to God, hears him say, "Satan, you incited *me* against him to ruin him without cause" (Job 2:3).

Do you understand what he is saying? God himself accepts the responsibility for what happened to Job. Although Satan is the one who carried it out, God accepts the responsibility. The very circumstances which Satan intended to be destructive in Job's life were the circumstances which God used redemptively in Job's life. And as you know, as a result of his adversity Job developed a greater piety. The very set of tragedies which Satan planned and instituted to elicit an evil response from Job (1:11) were the very circumstances which God engineered to produce greater maturity in Job. Thus one set of circumstances was at the same time a test and temptation.

Some difficult things may indeed come into your life— perhaps you've been cast off or laid off or otherwise abused. In any case, you need to recognize where these circumstances come from. Ultimately they come from God. He is the source of everything. He is a sovereign Lord. And he allows those things to come into your life in order to equip you to be his man or woman. But Satan is also active in those circumstances, and he intends for them to destroy your faith. Whether they are a test to build or a temptation to destroy depends upon your response.

James tells us that a circumstance becomes a temptation "when we are carried away and enticed by our own desire":

But each one is tempted when he is carried away and enticed by his own lust. Then when lust has conceived [i.e., when the will unites with the desire], it gives birth to sin; and when sin is accomplished, it brings forth death. Do not be deceived, my beloved brethren (James 1:14–16).

This is a very vivid analogy drawn from human conception and birth. Here is the way it works. An adverse circumstance comes into your life. If you submit to the Lord and turn to him, then that circumstance has become a test to strengthen you. But if you rebel against your circumstance, then sin is conceived and born. And sin then produces death—a sense of weakness, discouragement and defeat. But if we see that this circumstance, no matter how adverse it may be, comes from God, and if we accept it and lay hold of him and his life for deliverance, then the result is life. Notice verses 17 and 18:

Every good thing bestowed and every perfect gift is from above, coming down from the Father of lights, with whom there is no variation, or shifting shadow. In the exercise of His will He brought us forth by the word of truth, so that we might be as it were the first fruits among His creatures (James 1:17, 18).

That is, there is no darkness in God, no hidden, evil intentions. He wants the very best for us.

The proof that God is good is our own redemptive history. What has God done? Why, he brought us forth by the word of truth. We have a new life in Jesus Christ. We are the first fruits (the very best) of his creatures. Can he now have turned against us? Has he brought this circumstance into our life to destroy us? Of course not! He intends it for our good.

BE QUICK, BE SLOW

A fourth hindrance to joy is found in verse 19:

> This you know, my beloved brethren. But let every one be
> quick to hear, slow to speak and slow to anger; for the anger
> of man does not achieve the righteousness of God.

Quick to hear what? The word of truth. The fourth obsta-
cle to joy is our tendency to rebel against God's word in
times of stress. But James says, "Don't resist God. You
know that God is using his word in your life to produce
the best, so be *quick to hear* the word, be *slow to speak,* slow
to defend yourself, slow to justify yourself. And be *slow to
anger* against the people or the circumstances which are the
cause of your suffering. Because "the anger of man does not
achieve the righteousness of God." We know this well.

> Therefore putting aside all filthiness and all that remains of
> wickedness, in humility [setting aside our own rights] receive
> the word implanted, which is able to save your souls. But
> prove yourselves doers of the word, and not merely hearers
> who delude themselves [or who excuse themselves] (James
> 1:21, 22).

James says *hear the word.* When circumstances come into
your life to try you, your first response ought to be to
submit to God's word. Listen to it. And then receive it.
Perhaps James was thinking of Jesus' parable of the seed
and the sower. The ground which was responsive to the
word produced fruit, the measure of fruitfulness in each
case being the measure of receptivity. "So," he says, "receive the implanted word which is able to save your souls."
What is it, in times of stress, that most needs "saving"?
It is our *soul,* James points out. We know we are saved, that
is, justified before God, if we have received Jesus Christ.

But that is only the beginning. Throughout our lives God is at work in us to save our souls, to transform us in the areas of mind, emotions, and will. To the extent that we are victims of our emotions, or impulsiveness, or distorted perspectives, we are not living as kings. In times of pressure, our natural tendency is to make rash decisions, become angry, resentful, or self-pitying, or give way to discouragement and hopelessness. But James says that the implanted word, received in full awareness of our need, is able to slow us down, dispel our anger, and transform despair into hope.

But don't just receive the word; do it! Obey it. Respond to it. It is easy for us to avoid obedience by excusing our behavior. We can blame our wife or husband or boss or circumstances. And we can go on and on deluding ourselves and excusing ourselves and refusing to obey. The illustration James gives is very helpful:

For if any one is a hearer of the word and not a doer, he is like a man who looks at his natural face in a mirror; for once he has looked at himself and gone away, he has immediately forgotten what kind of person he was. But one who looks intently at the perfect law, the law of liberty and abides by it, not having become a forgetful hearer but an effectual doer, this man shall be blessed in what he does (James 1:23–25).

When I read this verse, it always takes me back to when my children were small. Whenever we asked them to wash their hands and faces they complied with a great deal of splashing about in the wash basin. But often they appeared for inspection with dirt on their faces, and looking as if they'd been out rooting with the pigs. We would say, "Boys, did you look in the mirror when you washed your face?" And they would say, "Sure!" But we knew they hadn't really taken a good look.

That is what James is saying. The man who casually glances at the word and looks away is like the man who looks in a mirror and sees that his face is dirty but goes away and does little or nothing about it. In contrast to that superficial splash we are to look *intently* into the word and give ourselves a good scrub. (The phrase *look intently* is used in John 20 to describe the people who came to the tomb where Jesus had been buried: They "stooped over and peered" into the dark tomb.) In other words, we ought to look carefully at *ourselves* as our lives are exposed by the word and do something about our soiled and smudged countenances: take seriously the defilement that we see there and wash ourselves thoroughly.

That word James describes as the perfect law—one exactly suited to our needs, and as the law that sets us free—free to be what we were meant to be. And he says when we determine to abide in it we are blessed (made happy or whole) in our doing—a beatitude James evidently recalled from Jesus' mouth: "If you know these things, you are blessed if you do them" (John 13:17). Obedience always carries with it a sense of joy and wholeness.

RESPONSE TO REVELATION

James now gives us a final word:

If any one thinks himself to be religious, and yet does not bridle his tongue but deceives his own heart, this man's religion is worthless. This is pure and undefiled religion in the sight of our God and Father, to visit orphans and widows in their distress, and to keep oneself unstained by the world (James 1:26, 27).

The word translated "religious" is the word which means essentially "to be worshipful." Worship is essentially a response to revelation. The word has been revealed, and we are to respond by obedience. True worship, thus, is obedience, and the marks of that worship are threefold. The first is a controlled tongue. The true worshiper has mastered his tongue. He doesn't under pressure verbally lash out at God, or men, or at his circumstances. James says in chapter 3 that we all stumble in many ways and "If any one does not stumble in what he says, he is a mature man, able to bridle the whole body as well." The tongue is an index of our level of spirituality. If you want to see where a man is spiritually, watch him under stress, and observe what he says. James says that if we are truly a doer of the word, our tongue will be under control.

The second mark of worship is found in verse 27. The true worshiper will visit widows and orphans in their distress. Why orphans and widows? Well, because this is the sort of quiet activity that no one appreciates. You get no kudos for calling on widows. No one sees or knows. But it is a mark of one who is not preoccupied by his own distress and thus can see and minister to the distress of others. If we have truly laid our cares upon Jesus Christ then we will not be concerned about our own struggles. We will think in terms of the needs of others and that concern will demonstrate itself in quiet acts of mercy.

And then a final mark of true worship is that one keeps himself from being stained by the world. The world is the community of flesh-governed people—the company of those who try to drug or distract themselves out of their sorrow and misery. But James says that the mark of a worshipful man is that he is unstained by that philosophy. In times of stress he finds strength in his God (Ps. 4:8).

This, then, is James' word about suffering. Suffering comes from God to perfect us, and it will do its work unless we hinder the process. God grant that we may allow the process to go on unimpeded so that we may be God's men and women, perfect and complete, lacking nothing.

3

The Triumph of Mercy

James 2:1–13

James 2:1–13 is essentially an attack on Christian snobbery. Such partiality, James reasons, is incompatible with faith in our Lord Jesus Christ. This is the theme that unifies the section. In the first verse he enunciates the principle in the form of a command. Verses 2–4 illustrate the principle; verses 5–11 further explain it. The final two verses (12, 13) are his conclusion to the matter.

First the statement of the principle:

My brethren, do not hold your faith in our glorious Lord Jesus Christ with an attitude of personal favoritism (James 2:1).

You will note that the verb is a command. Therefore, to discriminate on the basis of class or caste is sin. Or more to the point, no one can claim to believe in Jesus Christ and doggedly pursue a policy of discrimination based on birth, race, property or sex. The two positions are contradictory. I told you James doesn't mince his words. James contrasts faith in our glorious Lord Jesus Christ with personal favoritism. Our faith, which has for its object the Lord Jesus

Christ who reigns in heavenly glory, should teach us the worthlessness of evaluations based on mere earthly advantage. The Lord Jesus is the glorious one; all earthly glory pales in significance.

To show "personal favoritism" is literally to "receive by face" as in Leviticus 19:15 or estimate people on the basis of superficial characteristics—to receive by face (outward) rather than by heart (inward). Any time we reject someone because of the color of his skin or the length of his hair or the cut of his clothes, we violate this command. Conversely, when we embrace a brother on the same basis, we sin. Do you see the issue?

FOREIGN TO FAITH

And the reason such discrimination is precluded is because it is foreign to faith in Jesus Christ. The Lord himself does not discriminate on that basis. He never "received by face." This term occurs only four times in the New Testament (Rom. 2:11; Eph. 6:9; Col. 3:25; James 2:1). In every other instance God is the subject of the sentence, and it is stated emphatically that he does *not* "receive by face." There is a vivid Old Testament statement of this truth in 1 Samuel 16:7. The Lord said to the prophet Samuel regarding his choice of a king, "Do not look at his appearance or at the height of his stature . . . for God sees not as man sees, for man looks at the outward appearance, but the Lord looks at the heart." Do I then have another basis for judging a man? Can I refuse to accept and associate with one whom God has received?

I have been told that Gandhi, early in his career while he was in South Africa went to a Christian church where his English friend C. F. Andrews was to preach only to be turned away from the door because his skin was not white. How ironic that the opponent of caste in India was a victim of another caste system in a so-called Christian setting.

Perhaps our actions are not so contradictory to our faith. But are we not in attitude just as culpable? Any time we shrink from a brother because he is "not like us," we betray ourselves. The words of James are unequivocal. Prejudice is sin.

Now James illustrates out of their experience:

> For if a man comes into your assembly with a gold ring and dressed in fine clothes, and there also comes in a poor man in dirty clothes, and you pay special attention to the one who is wearing the fine clothes, and say, "You sit here in a good place," and you say to the poor man, "You stand over there, or sit down by my footstool" (James 2:2–4).

James selects a very pointed illustration. Such favoritism is particularly reprehensible when exhibited in a body of believers gathered for worship. That is certainly the place of all places to lay aside one's elitism. Yet they were discriminating against one another even there.

I mentioned earlier that James is an early writing, perhaps the earliest of all the New Testament books. One indication of that fact is James' reference here to worship in a synagogue ("assembly," v. 2). The term is not found elsewhere in the New Testament to describe a Christian congregation but always used of a building in which Jews worshiped. Therefore, the book must have been written early in the history of the church before they were ousted from the synagogues. This historical situation may shed some light on their actions. It may be that the Christians, feeling the mounting tension between the Christian and Jewish communities, were acting with partiality toward wealthy Jews in order to curry favor. Perhaps they felt that by rendering special honor to powerful Jewish civic leaders, they could stave off what appeared to be an imminent clash. But what they did not see was that in so doing, they

were dishonoring both the influential and their less prestigious brethren. And no matter what their ultimate intentions were, they were violating the spirit of the gospel.

The visitors described in verse 2 then would most likely
be influential members of the community who have come
to observe the meeting. The speaker in verse 3 is a member
of the congregation sitting in a comfortable seat provided
with a footstool. He rises and offers the wealthy stranger
his seat ("sit here in a good place") but contemptuously
gives the poor man a choice between standing "over there
[away from me]," or [if you must sit near me] sitting on the
floor. The well-dressed man is given preferential treatment. The shabbily dressed man is discriminated against.
You, James says, have judged with evil motives (or
thoughts).

The following section, then (vv. 5–11) explains why such
judgment is evil. Such discriminatory practices are wrong,
James reasons, because (1) they are contrary to God's choice
(v. 2:5); (2) they align one with the conduct of the unbeliev-
ing world (vv. 2:6–7) and (3) they are contrary to the commands of God's word (vv. 2:8–11).

GOD'S CHOICE

> Listen, my beloved brethren: did not God choose the poor of
> this world to be rich in faith and heirs of the kingdom which
> He promised to those who love Him? (James 2:5).

James declares that they have dishonored one whom God
has chosen *for himself* (for such is the import of the Greek
verb). It is a historical fact that the early church was largely
made up of the poorer classes. Paul commented that in his
day there were not many in the church who were politi-
cally powerful and of noble birth (1 Cor. 1:26). There were,
of course, a few who indeed had impressive credentials
such as Barnabas (Acts 4:36, 37), Lydia (Acts 16:14), and

Philemon, but it was largely the poor and wretched that flooded into the church.

One early opponent of Christianity rejected it as the "religion of all poor devils." But he was closer to the truth than he knew. Yet James does not say that God had to *settle* for the poor; rather he deliberately chose them for himself. They are special objects of his love. He embraces them. How can I reject them? Every member of the Body of Christ is there as a result of God's loving choice. He never asked me whom he should include in his Body. He has chosen Democrats as well as Republicans, the hip as well as the straight, the tall, dark and handsome and the short, shot and shapeless. How, then, can I exclude anyone from my home and table, my friendship and love whom God has called into fellowship with him?

If memory serves me well, I think I recall a couple of lines from a song that the Love Song (a Christian rock group) wrote a number of years ago:

> Long hair, short hair, some coats and ties
> Looking past the hair and straight into the eyes

That expresses well James' point about God's choice and our consequent response to those whom God has chosen.

And notice that he does not merely select the poor, he invests them with worth. He calls them to be rich in faith and joint heirs with Christ in his kingdom. Can I discriminate against a brother when he is a member of a royal family? Especially when I likewise have been adopted into that family through no merit of my own. To so judge is to reveal the evil in my heart.

THE CONDUCT OF THE UNGODLY

> But you have dishonored the poor man. Is it not the rich who oppress you and personally drag you into court? Do they not blaspheme the fair name by which you have been called? (James 2:6–7).

It is a matter of historical record that wealthy overlords preyed upon and exploited the early Jewish-Christian converts, as I have already mentioned. The rich are described here as those "who oppress [lord it over] you and personally drag you into court." They so controlled the courts that poor men could not secure justice—a complaint that has a contemporary ring. Furthermore, they (the rich) were blaspheming the "fair name" by which they were called (literally "which was called upon you"). The name is almost certainly the term *Christian* (one belonging to Christ) which was applied to those early believers, and which was being ridiculed and held up to scorn by their oppressors.

Now for the punch line. When, James reasons, you dishonor the poor man or the black man or any other minority member for that matter, you align yourself with their oppressors and have in effect adopted their hostile stance toward the Christian community. In short, you have identified yourself with the enemies of God.

THE COMMAND OF SCRIPTURE

If, however, you are fulfilling the royal law, according to the Scripture, "You shall love your neighbor as yourself," you are doing well. But if you show partiality, you are committing sin and are convicted by the law as transgressors. For whoever keeps the whole law and yet stumbles in one point, he has become guilty of all. For He who said, "Do not commit adultery," also said, "Do not commit murder." Now if you do not commit adultery, but do commit murder, you have become a transgressor of the law (James 2:8–11).

The third reason why such discrimination is wicked is that it's in violation of the word of God or as James describes it here, the *royal law*. That term was used by the Greek writers to refer to law that was enacted by duly constituted authority. In other words, it was a sovereign decree and therefore obligatory, not optional. James was, or so I believe, thinking not only of the Old Testament basis of this command (Lev. 19:18) but also Jesus' teaching recorded in Mark 12:31: "The second is this, 'You shall love your neighbor as yourself.' There is no other commandment greater than these."

The royal law then was the law of the King, the Lord Jesus—the law of love. It was Jesus who declared that the entire law could be reduced to one dictum—love your neighbor as yourself—a statement which the Apostle Paul echos in Romans 13:8–10:

> Owe nothing to anyone except to love one another; for he who loves his neighbor has fulfilled the law. For this, "You shall not commit adultery, you shall not murder, you shall not steal, you shall not covet," and if there is any other commandment, it is summed up in this saying, "You shall love your neighbor as yourself." Love does no wrong to a neighbor; love therefore is the fulfillment of the law.

Now let's see what James is getting at. His argument runs this way: Someone, in answer to his charge, might answer, "But by deferring to the influential man, I am in reality showing him love and thus I am fulfilling the command, "You shall love your neighbor as yourself" (Lev. 19:18). If that is your motive, James replies, you do well (James 2:8). But if you bestow honor on any man out of personal and private motives, if you "show partiality" (the verb form of the noun in verse 1, "receive by face"), you are not loving him at all. You, in fact, have violated the law of love and thus have broken the entire law of God. Obedience to one precept of the law is no excuse for disobedience to another. The breach of any command of the law is rebellion against the spirit of the law. To knowingly violate one law is like rebelling against the law in its entirety. The law is like a pane of glass. If I break one part of it, I have essentially broken it all.

Let me illustrate as James does (2:11). Suppose I say (and I believe this is precisely the way James is arguing) "I love you, and I will demonstrate my love by not committing adultery with your wife. However, I reserve the right to murder you next time you cross me. Three cheers for me!" I think that you would conclude that I have somehow missed the spirit of the law. Or, more to James' point, I have convicted myself of rebellion against the spirit of the law. It's obvious that I don't love you at all.

The law spells out the duties of love. If I truly love my brother, I will treat him according to *all* the dictates of the law. I will not commit adultery with his wife (Lev. 18:19), I will not murder him (Lev. 19:16), and (here it comes!) I will not evaluate him on the basis of his position or status in life (Lev. 19:15). In so doing, I will love my neighbor as myself. "Loves does no wrong to a neighbor; love therefore is the fulfillment of the law" (Rom. 13:10).

James is very clear. To discriminate against anyone on the basis of color, sex or social status is a violation of the law of love. Prejudice is a sin. Do we esteem all men as highly as God does? The Bible says that we owe love to every man. We are in debt to *every man*. We cannot selectively reduce that debt.

This Is Love

One further note about love. It's a difficult concept to explain. Scripture never gives us a textbook or dictionary definition of love. In the New Testament, God directs us to look at himself, or to look at his Son, if we want to see what love is. John says, "This is love, not that we loved God but that he loved us and sent his Son to be the expiation for our sins." That is what love is—it is the giving of yourself. Paul says in Ephesians 5 that husbands are to love their wives "as Christ loved the church and gave himself up for her." That is the nature of the love that we receive from Jesus Christ. It isn't dependent upon the lovableness of the people who are the objects of that love, nor upon any external feature which would naturally draw us to them.

One of my young student friends once wrote a poem about his girlfriend. It's called, "My Girl." Any resemblance between the subject of this poem and persons living or dead is purely coincidental.

> Steve's girl is rich and haughty;
> My girl is poor as clay.
> Steve's girl is young and pretty;
> My girl looks like a bale of hay.
> Steve's girl is smart and clever;
> My girl is dumb, but good.
> But would I trade my girl for Steve's?
> You bet your life I would!

Doesn't that tug at your heart strings? Well not exactly. Especially if you look like a bale of hay. But isn't it good to know that God loves you even if you do? He does not judge by face or form. He *unconditionally* loves you. And that establishes the nature of our love for others. His love is made available to us to love the unlovely. He is, in fact, the source of all genuine love. "Beloved, let us love one another for love is from God; and every one who loves is born of God and knows God" (1 John 4:7).

The next two verses of this chapter record James' conclusion:

> So speak and so act, as those who are to be judged by the law of liberty. For judgment will be merciless to one who has shown no mercy; mercy triumphs over judgment (James 2: 12–13).

Verse 4 reveals that evil thoughts determine what one *says* and does. Now James calls for a new way of thinking—

the law of liberty, and he insists that we speak *and* act according to that standard. There is no reason to think that James is contrasting Old Testament law with some milder and less strict form of New Testament teaching. James is still thinking about the Old Testament proscription of prejudicial action against a brother (e.g., Lev. 19:15). The point is simply that true liberty is doing God's will. Disobedience results in bondage. Obedience sets us free.

Jesus said, "Everyone who commits sin is the slave of sin" (John 8:34). The violation of God's will, therefore, is doubly reprehensible. It is both an offense against God and ourselves. Obedience, on the other hand, sets us free—free from our pride and prejudice. Hence the title, The Law of Liberty.

James calls his readers to speak and act according to that standard because we are being judged by it, and that judgment will be merciless to the one who shows no mercy. In other words, if we show no spirit of mercy to an unattractive brother, then we will be shown no mercy in the judgment—a sobering thought to be sure! These are stern words, but no more stern than the words of Jesus when he commented upon this same matter:

Then Peter came and said to Him, "Lord, how often shall my brother sin against me and I forgive him? Up to seven times?" Jesus said to him, "I do not say to you, up to seven times, but up to seventy times seven. For this reason the kingdom of heaven may be compared to a certain king who wishes to settle accounts with his slaves. And when he had begun to settle them, there was brought to him one who owed him ten thousand talents. But since he did not have the means to repay, his lord commanded him to be sold, along with his wife and children and all that he had, and repayment to be made. The slave therefore falling down, prostrated himself before him, saying, 'Have patience with me, and I will repay you everything.' And

the lord of that slave felt compassion and released him and
forgave him the debt. But that slave went out and found one
of his fellow-slaves who owed him a hundred denarii; and he
seized him and began to choke him, saying, 'Pay back what
you owe.' So his fellow-slave fell down and began to entreat
him, saying, 'Have patience with me and I will repay you.' He
was unwilling however, but went and threw him in prison
until he should pay back what was owed. So when his fellow-
slaves saw what had happened, they were deeply grieved and
came and reported to their lord all that had happened. Then
summoning him, his lord said to him, 'You wicked slave, I
forgave you all that debt because you entreated me. Should
you not also have had mercy on your fellow-slave, even as I
had mercy on you?' And his lord, moved with anger, handed
him over to the torturers until he should repay all that was
owed him. So shall My heavenly Father also do to you, if each
of you does not forgive his brother from your heart" (Matt.
18:21–35).

Now we need to be clear about what both James and
Jesus are saying. They are not suggesting that mercy has
any purchasing power. It does not somehow obligate God
to show us mercy. The mercy that we show is merely
evidential. It demonstrates that we understand the basis of
our own acceptance before God. If we fully understand the
depth of our own need for mercy, we will extend it to
others. If we are not merciful, we indicate that we do not
realize how much we ourselves have been forgiven. That
is what is behind Jesus' comment to Peter and the demand
for infinite forgiveness. (This is what we should infer from
the seventy-times-seven equation.) Peter's natural inclina-
tion (and ours) was to establish a finite limit to the number
of offenses a man can endure. Seven times, and then we've
had it! Jesus says in effect that forgiveness and mercy have
no limits. There is never a time when we can legitimately
say "I've had enough" or "That's the last straw." Because

God himself never treats us that way; he has forgiven us *all* our transgressions. The hymn states it well:

> His love knows no limits
> His grace has no measure
> His power has no bound'ry known unto men
> For out of his infinite riches in glory,
> He giveth, and giveth, and giveth again.

Therefore, when we are merciful to the unlovely and obnoxious, it is because we have recognized our own unloveliness to God and need for forgiveness, and we have become a child of God. Thus mercy triumphs over judgment.

I'm sure you've noticed by now that God has called a very diverse and heterogeneous group into his family. They come in all sizes, shapes and colors. They live on your block and across the tracks. Some don't dress like you do or smell like you do. Some, they tell me, even wear a bone in their nose. Yet, "red and yellow, black and white they are precious in *his* sight." Are they precious to you?

4

True Faith

James 2:14–26

I mentioned earlier that the primary thrust of this letter is a merciless attack on hypocrisy. It is also, however, by clear implication, a practical and encouraging description of true faith. If Christ is really Lord, then the marks of his lordship will appear in our lives. James recognizes that men can be easily deceived in these matters, as he himself once was when his older brother lived in his own house, un-recognized as the Lord of his life. But the word of God, he has told us, is like a mirror in which we become un-deceived, as we are shown what we are really like. The writer to the Hebrews says, "The word of God is living and active and sharper than any two-edged sword, and piercing as far as the division of soul and spirit, of both joints and marrow, and able to judge the thoughts and intentions of the heart" (Heb. 4:12). It is just such a living, active, sharp, piercing, discerning word that we have here. It is meant to reveal the reality of our lives that lies beneath the words we speak. God does not hide the truth from us, waiting behind the scenes for us to fail, so that he can pounce on us in the day of judgment. He is merciful; he yearns for us to know the truth about ourselves *now*, so that he can give us full and productive lives and conform us to the image of Christ.

This brings us to the central issue of this section: true faith is purposeful, productive, and visible. The first part, verses 14 through 20, is the negative statement, a description of what faith is *not*. Then, in verses 21 through 25, James gives us the positive description of faith, using helpful illustrations from Scripture to amplify his point. First, the negative:

> What use is it, my brethren, if a man says he has faith, but he has no works? Can that faith save him? (James 2:14).

Faith without works is useless. Or, to put it another way, true faith is, by its nature, useful. Useful for what? James seems to indicate that it is designed to *save* us. Well, we already know that we are saved by faith, but James makes it clear that there is an essential element, without which our faith cannot save us, because it is not true faith. It is the element of works, the activity that comes from faith. James makes the distinction here between what a man says he believes and how his belief behaves. If the two don't jibe, we can't believe what he says.

James may have had in mind Jesus' words to the scribes and Pharisees on one occasion. They spoke with knowledge of the Law of Moses, Jesus said, "Therefore all that they tell you, do and observe, but do not do according to their deeds; for they say things, and do not do them. And they tie up heavy loads, and lay them on men's shoulders; but they themselves are unwilling to move them with so much as a finger" (Matt. 23:3–4).

Do you remember how Jesus responded to Philip when he said, "Lord, show us the Father." Jesus answered, "Have I been so long with you, and yet you have not come to know

Me, Philip? . . . Believe Me that I am in the Father, and
the Father in Me; otherwise believe on account of the
works themselves" (John 14:8–11). It was the works as well
as the words that reflected the true character of the Son of
God.

James goes on now to explain what he means:

> If a brother or sister is without clothing and in need of daily
> food, and one of you says to them, "Go in peace, be warmed
> and be filled"; and yet you do not give them what is necessary
> for their body; what use is that? Even so faith, if it has no
> works, is dead, being by itself (James 2:15–17).

This is an analogy, not an accusation; James says, "Suppose
a brother comes to you for help. He has been out of work
for months, and he's at the end of his tether. He's cold and
hungry. Will you say to him, 'Go in peace, be warmed and be
filled; I'll pray for you'?" Of course not. What good
would your pious words do in meeting his bodily needs?
"Even so," James says, "of what use is your faith if it
doesn't produce results? It is useless, being by itself."

Two Kinds of "Works"

What does James mean by "works"? Before we go any
farther, we need to understand the difference between
works as James uses the word and *works* as Paul uses it in
Romans. Paul says, "A man is justified by faith apart from
works of the Law" (Rom. 3:28). The kind of works he is
talking about there is "works of the Law." All have sinned
and fallen short of the perfect standard of God's law. No
one can, by trying, perfectly obey the law—even in its
external aspects—and especially not in the area of our attitudes. There is nothing man can do, no work or activity
of his own, that can bring him into a right relationship
with God. One can never pull himself up by his own boot-

straps. There is only one way by which we can have access to God, and that way is through faith in Jesus. Jesus is the Way.

But faith is a way of life, a living expression, or outworking, of what we believe. James is saying that if our faith is not producing—if it is not fruitful—then we need to take a hard look at what we call our faith. The Scriptures are filled with this teaching. In Isaiah 58, the same idea is powerfully expressed. Here the prophet has been speaking out against the religious way of life the people were leading, with publicly demonstrated ritual fasts, and he says God has paid no attention to their prayers because they have missed the whole idea behind the ritual:

> "Is this not the fast which I chose,
> To loosen the bonds of wickedness,
> To undo the bands of the yoke,
> And to let the oppressed go free,
> And break every yoke?
> Is it not to divide your bread with the hungry,
> And bring the homeless poor into the house;
> When you see the naked, to cover him;
> And not to hide yourself from your own flesh?"
>
> (Isa. 58:6–7).

James himself said earlier, "Pure and undefiled religion [is] to visit orphans and widows in their distress." That is where God's heart is. Faith is purposeful and productive. Also, it is visible:

> But someone may well say, "You have faith, and I have works; show me your faith without the works, and I will show you my faith by my works" (James 2:18).

If a brother should hear your claim to faith, he may well say, "Show me." He has a right to expect to see evidence of your faith; it is by your actions that your faith is made visible. Faith is a way of walking in dependence on Jesus Christ, instead of on any other visible entity. In the old movie classic *The Invisible Man*, the only way people knew he was in the area was if he moved things around. A book would float up off the table, or a coffee cup would be drained into thin air, or a curious depression would appear in the sofa cushion as he sat down. In the same way, the presence of true faith is made known to other people only by what it *does*, in terms of changes in a person's perspectives, values, and activities.

Now James lets go with both barrels:

> You believe that God is one. You do well; the demons also believe, and shudder. But are you willing to recognize, you foolish fellow, that faith without works is useless? (James 2:19 20).

The Jewish believers who read this would undoubtedly think immediately of Moses' proclamation recorded in Deuteronomy: "Hear, O Israel! The Lord is our God, the Lord is one!" (Deut. 6:4). But, James says, mere acknowledgment of God's existence as the only living God is not enough. Demons also believe that, but it doesn't change their demonic character; they are not the friends of God. It isn't abstract theology that counts for anything, and James says that anyone who thinks that way is foolish, without wisdom.

Now, he turns to a positive statement of what faith *is:* "Was not Abraham our father justified by works, when he offered up Isaac his son on the altar?" (James 2:21). James refers to Abraham here as "our father." It was, of course, customary for Jews to refer to Abraham as their "father," but in the context of his discussion on true faith, James is emphasizing the fact that Abraham was the father of all who believed, whether circumcised or not, as Paul points out in Romans. James and Paul both use Abraham to illustrate the same basic principle—Paul from the theological point of view, and James from the practical, "so what" perspective: Abraham believed God, and therefore was justified.

FRUITFUL FAITH

But how do we *know* he believed? Was it because he said so? Would that have made any impression on us, or caused the apostles to use him as an example? Of course not. The reason Abraham is such a powerful example is that his faith bore fruit. He trusted God *for* something. He actually walked up that mountain, built an altar, placed his beloved son on it, kindled the fire, and raised the knife of slaughter. He knew that God's promise to multiply Abraham's descendants was centered in Isaac, but he offered Isaac on the altar in obedience to God. And God provided a substitute sacrifice for Isaac.

> You see that faith was working with his works, and as a result of the works, faith was perfected; and the Scripture was fulfilled which says, "And Abraham believed God, and it was reckoned to him as righteousness," and he was called the friend of God (James 2:22 23).

As a result of Abraham's *work* of faith, his faith was perfected. That means that God proved himself to be faithful, and Abraham had a rock-certain basis for continuing in faith. His faith was confirmed. This is not to imply that at this moment in his life he was justified. He had responded many times before in faith to what God asked him to do. He was experienced in walking by faith, but it was his obedience that made his faith complete. God had prepared him for this moment, just as he prepares us, step by step, as we respond to one request after another. As we learn of his faithfulness, learn to trust him as sovereign Lord, we are made perfect in faith.

So many times, we wish God would work the other way around. We wish he would show us the ram hidden in the bushes first, and then we would be willing to do whatever he asks. But the truth is that faith is made strong only by acting in obedience, when there is no evidence of God being anywhere around, and that then we will be justified. Our faith, acting on God's promise, will be confirmed, and we will not be ashamed of having trusted in an invisible God.

Abraham was called "the friend of God." That is what it means to be justified. We can come freely into the presence of God and converse with him; our lives are open to him—as to any good friend—and he is totally caring and available to us, willing to share his plans with us. Jesus said to his disciples just before he went to the cross, "No longer do I call you slaves; for the slave does not know what his master is doing; but I have called you friends" (John 15:15). It is extraordinary that his act of friendship—laying down his life for us—can make us *his* friends; although I can see how it should make him *our* friend. Anyway, it is by faith, working with our works, that we are called friends of God. "You see," concludes James, "that a man is justified by works, and not by faith alone" (James 2:24).

A DUBIOUS CANDIDATE

The second illustration from Scriptures to describe true faith is a very pointed one:

> And in the same way was not Rahab the harlot also justified by works, when she received the messengers and sent them out by another way? (James 2:25).

Rahab was a prostitute and a Canaanite who lived in Jericho at the time of the conquest. To any self-respecting Jew, such a woman would be a very dubious candidate for inclusion in the family of God. By using Rahab as an example of the kind of faith that is able to save us, James is taking a swipe at any remaining tendency among the Jewish Christians toward elitism. Heritage, ancestry, background, family connection—none of these mean anything to God. His eye is on the one—anyone—who trusts him. Abraham was counted righteous because of his faith, and not because of his status. Rahab also was counted righteous, because she believed. She is no second-class citizen, either; she ranks with Abraham.

The other thing that is noteworthy in this brief reference to Rahab is the nature of what she did. In some ways, her actions were very similar to Abraham's, but the contrast is more striking than the similarity. Whereas Abraham knew that the entire fate of future generations, promised through Isaac, was at stake, Rahab was concerned about herself and her family. For her, the situation was critical. Confronted with probable annihilation by the Israelites, and having heard of the amazing things the Lord had already done on their behalf, she was impressed and rightly afraid. The fear of the Lord was definitely upon her. This is one very common way the Lord uses to drive people to transfer their dependence to him. And this is exactly what Rahab did; she heard the truth about God, and she believed, and on the basis of her belief she acted. She received the two spies, hiding them on her roof at the risk of her own life, and when the coast was clear she sent them on their way, trusting her life to them. They were total strangers to her. Not only they, but God also was a stranger to her. She had not walked with God before, had no long experience of faith behind her, but she trusted him to save her.

I think her act of simple faith is a picture to us of the way we must first come to Christ. There is no need to tidy up our lives before we put our trust in him. We don't have to get "gussied up" first—in fact, there is no point in doing so, because we cannot. Only Jesus is able to deal with the way we are, the habits and attitudes that are deeply ingrained in us.

I know a busy homemaker who hires a woman to come in and help clean her house every Thursday. On Wednesday, she races frantically around picking up dirty clothes, washing the dishes, sweeping the floor and emptying the trash. I asked once why she went to all that trouble, since that was what she had hired the cleaning lady to do, and she said, "Oh, I couldn't look her in the face if she saw the apartment in such a mess!" It was useless for me to point out that it was her cleaning lady's job to tidy up the place.

I'm sure I don't need to press the analogy, except to say that it is our Lord's job to clean up our lives. It is simply wasted energy and pride to try to do it on our own. So Rahab, a woman of questionable respectability, simply put herself in God's hands. As a result she was saved and included in the Israelite community because she acted in faith.

Perhaps James is suggesting to his readers by this that not only should they show no partiality to rich people, or proper Jews, but they should also not be condescending to new believers. It is often those who are newborn in Christ who will be a source of refreshment and renewal to older Christians. They have a startling and ingenious way of asking very pointed questions, which can stir up older believers to a new perspective on what may have become a faith encrusted with religious traditions.

James concludes the chapter with this final word: "For just as the body without the spirit is dead, so also faith without works is dead" (James 2:26).

This simple analogy shows us the absolutely integral relationship between works and faith. The life of the body is the spirit—that is, the breath. In the same way, the life of faith is the works of faith. Without the spirit, the body would be lifeless, and without works, faith is no more viable than a corpse.

Having sorted out something of what James says in this passage, we need to make sure we understand what he *means*. James is writing this letter to believers, or rather, to those who have professed to believe in Christ as their Savior. Anyone who claims to believe in him should be behaving in such a way that Christ will be evident, visibly at work in that person's life. The distinction is between a belief that says all the right things and a belief that behaves.

But what if we, who know that we are born again into Christ, are not able to read this passage without squirming? I often feel, when I read this, as though James is holding me by the scruff of the neck, trying to shake some sense into me—for my own good, of course. But to James, understanding this passage is a question of our salvation, and that is worth everything to him. On one level, it is salvation in terms of initial justification and reconciliation with God through faith in Jesus Christ. Some who think they are saved show by their lives that they are only mouthing religious words. For them, the answer, of course, is to come to Jesus and believe in him.

Free to Choose

On another level, however, and the most important one in this context, salvation means the *process* of saving our souls, which is possible only through daily submitting ourselves to the word of God and, by the Spirit, applying what it says to our lives. Paul, in his letter to the Galatians, puts it this way: "If we live by the Spirit [that is, if the Spirit is the source of our life], let us also walk by the Spirit [daily, moment by moment, making the choices that accord with the new life we have in Christ]" (Gal. 5:25). The trouble with Christianity is that we are still free to choose. We are never forced to do what God desires; we are always left free to make choices for him. James' purpose is to enlist our willing cooperation with what God desires to do in our lives.

Therefore, how shall we respond to James' word here? Perhaps the most obvious, natural response would be guilt, followed by a flurry of good works. But I don't think James is suggesting that we do this, because he is discussing works related to *faith*. Anything we do out of a sense of duty, or even out of a desire to please God, is not a work of faith.

I remember a wonderful monologue recorded by comedian Bill Cosby on the unbearable anticipation a child feels on the night before Christmas. When he was a boy, he figured that the only thing to do was to go to bed early and go to sleep; that way Christmas morning would come more quickly. So he and his brother would turn in about four o'clock in the afternoon. At this point in his story, Cosby paused significantly and said, "Did you ever really *try* and go to sleep? Nothing!" That is exactly the way it is with us when we try to do good works. We can have the best intentions in the world, and the whole thing will be absolutely worthless as a demonstration of God's life and love in us. What it *will* be, will be a demonstration of ourselves, and sooner or later, we will break down under the strain of trying to be good.

James is exhorting us, I believe, to examine our lives critically, in the light of the truth. This does not mean that we should go around peering at our insides all the time— that is a sure way to stumble and fall. It does mean, though, that there is a time for careful, frank evaluation before God, without self-condemnation, but with a view to becoming the person God wants us to be. Upon examination, we are bound to find areas of weakness of faith. We will discover fearfulness in the face of certain demands, perhaps. Or unwillingness to get involved with someone who needs help. Or irritability toward our family. Whatever it is that God shows us in these times, we must recognize first that only God has the power to deal with them; second, we must choose to let him deal with them; and third, we are to *act* on our decision to trust God. We are to count on him to provide the necessary strength, wisdom, patience, or whatever, to do what he asks us to do. Our response must derive from a great "therefore"; because God first loved us, *therefore* we love. That kind of obedience will result in the perfecting of our faith and will also be a beacon to the world around us, revealing the glory of God.

5

The Teacher, the Tongue,
and Two Kinds of Wisdom

James 3:1–18

True faith is demonstrable. You can see it at work. That is the inescapable conclusion James has drawn us to. It issues in poise under pressure (James 1:2–12), and power to carry out quiet acts of love for all classes of humanity (James 1:26–2:13). For James, a faith that does not issue in action is not only dead (James 2:26), it is downright demonic: "You believe that God is one. You do well; the demons also believe, and shudder" (James 2:19).

Chapter 3, I believe, picks up this theme and applies it to a specific situation—teachers in local assemblies. The chapter division unfortunately obscures that connection. It may well be that James' treatment on the relationship between faith and works (James 2:14–26) is the theological basis for this practical appeal. Similarly, the Apostle Paul's lengthy discourse on the self-emptying of Christ (Phil. 2: 1–11) is the necessary theological base for his appeal to Euodia and Syntyche to lay aside their rights and stop quarreling. In fact it may be that the entire Book of Philippians, with its profound insight into the person of Christ, was written entirely with these two quarrelsome ladies in mind. Theology, you realize, has just that sort of practicality to it. These great truths are truths to live by. The goal of all Bible study and reading, then, is not to master these great themes, but rather to be mastered by them. This being the case, James 2:14–26, with its mind-boggling insights, may have been written with the situation in chapter 3 in mind. In fact, I believe it was. Follow along with me.

The author introduces his subject in this way: "Let not many of you become teachers, my brethren, knowing that as such we shall incur a stricter judgment" (James 3:1). Literally he says, "Stop becoming teachers" (evidently many were!). Doesn't it strike you odd that James would so interdict teaching? That ministry was needed then as now. Certainly the gift of teaching was and continues to be a legitimate and necessary function within a working body of believers. Teachers are essential. Why would he prohibit people from exercising this vital activity?

The answer, of course, is that he is not prohibiting the exercise of this gift. A quick look at the rest of the chapter indicates that he is only sounding a precautionary note. Teaching, then as now, was a prestigious position in the church. The teachers of Israel were highly regarded and often venerated long after their deaths. The Aramaic word *Rabbi*, applied to their teachers, actually means "my great one." Rabbis were not only doctors of the law, but leaders in their communities, treated with great honor and respect. It is inevitable, therefore, that in the early church their teachers would likewise be held in high regard. It was a highly desirable position. Evidently then men in the congregation were aspiring to that high office and doing so without due regard for the responsibility that the position entailed. It is that unthinking ambition about which James is speaking. In other words, he wants teachers to be duly aware of the moral responsibility involved in a teaching ministry. It is not something to be taken up carelessly.

His argument proceeds in this way: Teachers have greater responsibility not because of the greater honor of their office, but rather because of their greater vulnerability. Teachers teach through two channels: by what they say (the tongue) and by what they are (their behavior). Men teach by both speech and life, and it is those two areas in which teachers are most prone to failure. Thus I would construct the passage along the following lines: (1) The warning, James 3:1; (2) the reasons for the warning, James 3:2–18— a. the nature of the tongue, 3:2–12; b. the nature of true wisdom, 3:13–18.

Now let's review the historical situation again. Men in the early church were clamoring to become teachers because of the prestige and perquisites that the office provided. James restrains them: "Let not many of you become teachers, my brethren, knowing that as such we shall incur a stricter judgment" (James 3:1). Teachers deal with the most precious commodity in the world—a human life. As my friend Bob Smith says, "People are God's most important product." God places people into our hands to form and shape, and anyone mishandling or abusing that trust will bring down judgment on himself.

Happily, James is not referring here to a final judgment or condemnation. The Authorized Version's "condemnation" is far too strong. James' warning has to be viewed in the context of this chapter. He is addressing himself to *believers* whose destiny is fixed and secure. However, they needed to be reminded that as God's people they would still appear before the judgment seat of Christ to "be recompensed for deeds done in the body . . . whether good or bad" (2 Cor. 5:10). Every believer has to face that accounting. And that ought to sober us and motivate us to act according to the truth (2 Cor. 5:11).

Note that James includes himself in this warning: *"We*

shall incur a stricter judgment" (James 3:1). James was a teacher in the church at Jerusalem, and one of the "pillars" of that group of believers. He was known for his power and piety. Yet he recognizes that even he can lose perspective and misuse his teaching office. Alas, the flesh is always with us. We never outgrow it. The flesh may have died with Christ, but that's only true to faith. Old flesh (apart from Christ) never dies. It just smells that way. And there is nothing quite so malodorous as teachers who have forgotten James' warning in this passage. Even James senses the need to be subject to it.

THE TELLTALE TONGUE

Now James turns to the matter of the tongue.

> For we all stumble in many ways. If any one does not stumble in what he says, he is a perfect man, able to bridle the whole body as well (James 3:2).

I've often thought I was born with a silver foot in my mouth. I have no trouble identifying with James' critique of the tongue. There are many ways to stumble or trip in this life, but mostly we sin by what we say. Actually James takes the matter one step further. He is not merely saying that we are sinful in what we say. He is rather saying that what we say shows how sinful we are! The tongue tells on us. It is an accurate index of our spiritual condition as it apparently is of our physical well-being. Countless times I've been asked to stick out my tongue in a doctor's office. I've never known what it is about my tongue that tips him off to the state of my health, but it must reveal something. He always takes a good look at it, and so it is in the realm of the spirit. The tongue is the measure of the spiritual life of the man.

Now I want to be clear that he is *not* saying that maturity is measured merely by our ability to control our tongue.

In other words, one is not mature simply because he can discipline himself to always say the right things at the right time—he can quash angry and harsh words before they pass his lips, or suppress the desire to tell an obscene story or let fly with a round oath. In fact James reveals that such self-control is impossible. If suppression is the index of maturity, we will never measure up. To the contrary, as James will say later, the tongue will not be caged or mastered. It is a thoroughly incorrigible member of our body and will always slip out from under our control.

What James does point out, however, is that if we are truly mature and under the control of God, then our tongues will reveal that fact. When God has bridled the entire life, then the tongue is bridled. Thus when the tongue is bridled it is an indicator of the measure of Lordship Christ is exercising in our members. Do you understand how he is arguing? The tongue tells all. We may fool some of the people (and ourselves) some of the time, but sooner or later our tongue will betray us and everyone will know what we are *really* like within. That is a sobering thought indeed.

May I illustrate from my own experience? There are certain people who bring out the worst in me (that's the way I put it). Actually, I am a very placid, loving, generous, person. If I still lived in Texas they'd call me a "good ol' boy." However, there are certain people who always "make" me mad. They create irritability and hostility in me. It's their fault, you see. I am actually quite nice and easy to live with. So I try to be nice. And it works for awhile until I am pushed beyond the limit of self-control, and then my tongue betrays me. To my astonishment I am not nice at all. I am, in fact, downright mean and ornery. My tongue has found me out. I can no longer prolong the notion that I am a mature man.

That likewise was David's conclusion:

> I said, "I will guard my ways,
> That I may not sin with my tongue;
> I will guard my mouth as with a muzzle,
> While the wicked are in my presence."
> I was dumb and silent,
> I refrained even from good;
> And my sorrow [pain] grew worse.
> My heart was hot within me;
> While I was musing the fire burned;
> Then I spoke with my tongue:
> "Lord, make me to know my end,
> And what is the extent of my days,
> Let me know how transient [lacking] I am."
> Psalm 39:1–4

The tongue, therefore, is an important member. It reveals what we are. It is, in fact, the measure of our manhood.

The three illustrations that follow underscore the importance of the tongue:

> Now if we put the bits into the horses' mouths so that they may obey us, we direct their entire body as well.
>
> Behold, the ships also, though they are so great and are driven by strong winds, are still directed by a very small rudder, wherever the inclination of the pilot desires.
>
> So also the tongue is a small part of the body, and yet it boasts of great things. Behold, how great a forest is set aflame by such a small fire! (James 3:3–5).

Little Things Mean a Lot

Powerful horses are controlled by small bits in their mouths. The great merchant ships of James' day, though driven by winds of great force, were nevertheless maneuvered by means of the small movements of the helm. So, James reasons, the tongue, though it is a small member in the body, accomplishes great things. And then almost as

an afterthought, James notes the far-ranging effects of a
small fire. An unattended campfire or, in our day, a match
tossed carelessly aside can result in a terrible conflagration
and the devastation of vast stands of timber. Little things
can mean a lot.

A friend of mine was riding his motorcycle down a free-
way when a bug flew into his mouth. He was so astonished
that he lost control of his bike and ran head-on into a
cement overpass support. Fortunately he survived and ultimately recovered completely, though he spent the next six
months in traction. However, he learned a vital lesson:
Little things can have a great impact on your life! And,
James argues, the tongue is one of them.

Have you learned that truth? The tongue can do awe-
some things. It can devastate entire areas of life. Like a
runaway forest fire, it can irreparably damage a life. A
hasty word can destroy a reputation or undermine one's
confidence in a brother. So many times we allow words to
slip out of our mouths which, once spoken, we would do
anything to retract. But they have already taken effect.
There is something about the impact of words that is almost ineradicable. They cannot be unsaid, and after even
the most heartfelt apology the sting endures.

Or quite apart from the disastrous effect of harsh and
angry words, our tongues can influence others to do evil.
Whole nations have been inflamed by a few well-contrived
words. The tongue has potential for both good and evil. It
can radically affect the course of both individuals and nations. That seems to be what James has in mind when he
describes the far-reaching influence of the tongue:

And the tongue is a fire, the very world of iniquity; the tongue
is set among our members as that which defiles the entire
body, and sets on fire the course of our life, and is set on fire
by hell (James 3:6).

The tongue, to James, represents the evil world. The tongue is an evil microcosm. All the wickedness in the entire world finds its expression in the tongue. Malice, greed, anger, lust, hostility, avarice, pride, etc.—the tongue will suggest it or condone it.

Furthermore, the tongue defiles the entire body and sets on fire the course of life. Both the totality of our being and the duration of our lives are affected by it. There is never any part of our personality nor any part of this globe where we can go to escape it. Nor do we ever outgrow it.

The tongue is with us every moment of our lives. From the first cries of infancy to the crankiness of old age it influences both us and others. It sets on fire the course of our life. It reflects the awkwardness of youth and irrascibility of old age. It burns its way through our entire life like an out-of-control forest fire, leaving behind devastation and ruin. It is indeed, as James observes, a hellish thing.

OUT OF THE GARBAGE DUMP

James' word for hell in verse 6 is striking. It is a word frequently used by Jesus, but infrequently used by the apostles. It is the word *Gehenna* which you may know was a geographical site well known in James' day. Gehenna, or the Valley of Hinnom (the original owners) was the garbage dump of Jerusalem. It was located just to the southwest of the city and early in its history was associated with many of the terrible idolatrous practices of the Israelite monarchy. It was the seat of the worship of Molech to whom children were sacrificed. On account of these practices, the place was defiled by good king Josiah (2 Kings 23:10) and became in consequence a symbol of defilement. Shortly afterwards the valley became a dumping ground for the refuse from the city of Jerusalem—associated with fire and filth and symbolic of hell, presided over by Baalzebub, the Lord of the Flies (2 Kings 1:2, 3, 16). What a graphic metaphor for describing the source of our speech. Where does the filth that rolls off our tongues come from? From the cosmic garbage dump! How grimly descriptive that is!

But the picture becomes even more bleak:

> For every species of beasts and birds, of reptiles and creatures of the sea, is tamed, and has been tamed by the human race. But no one can tame the tongue; it is a restless evil and full of deadly poison (James 3:7–8).

No one can tame the tongue. Every species of bird and beast is currently being tamed or at some point in history has been tamed. That seems difficult to imagine, but James vouches for it. However, no man has ever tamed the tongue; it is restless and venomous, savage and incorrigible.

THE INCONGRUITY OF A DOUBLE-MINDED TONGUE

In verses 9 through 12 James describes the baffling, incongruous conduct of the tongue:

> With it we bless our Lord and Father; and with it we curse men, who have been made in the likeness of God; from the same mouth come both blessing and cursing. My brethren, these things ought not to be this way. Does a fountain send out from the same opening both fresh and bitter water? Can a fig tree, my brethren, produce olives, or a vine produce figs? Neither can salt water produce fresh (James 3:9–12).

How can we bless God in one breath and curse men made in the image of God in the next? Why do we speak gracious words to those we love the most and then, in a moment of rage and frustration, lash out at them? Why do we speak tenderly to our children at one time and then with harshness at another? Who can explain this strange ambivalence?

CONSIDER THE SOURCE

The illustrations used by James give us the answer to the baffling behavior of the tongue. If you observed a fountain producing fresh water one moment and brackish the next it would occur to you that something was happening there which was contrary to nature. The same conclusion could be applied to James' similar metaphor of the fig tree. A fresh spring does not produce salt water. Fig trees do not produce olives. Such products would be totally contrary to the nature of things. And that is precisely James' point. Our tongue reveals that something contrary to nature is at work in man. It reveals, in fact, that of all of God's creation man alone acts unnaturally. His actions can and do proceed from more than one fountainhead or source. He expresses that fact most eloquently. Our tongues, in effect, indicate the source of control in our lives. Kind words indicate one source, harsh words another. Truthful words are emitted from one source, lies from another. James is, in fact, going back to the first point made in this discussion: the tongue tells on us. It reveals our state of being. Just as the fuzz on my tongue reveals the general state of my physical health, so my spiritual state of being is indicated by my tongue. If I am controlled and ordered by the Spirit of God, my tongue will reflect that reliance. If I am not, you can detect that fact from what I say. The tongue, therefore, is a most accurate indicator of the measure of my manhood in Christ. If my speech is edifying, encouraging, uplifting, then it is because the Lord Jesus has harnessed my entire body for his purposes. But if cursing and bitterness proceed from my mouth, I am demonstrating that I am operating under the rule of the flesh. Jesus said, "Out of the abundance of the heart the mouth speaks" (Matt. 12:34, RSV).

TWO KINDS OF WISDOM

James now turns to the second measure of a teacher—the wisdom displayed through his behavior. Teachers not only teach by exhortation, but also by example. Here, as with the tongue, responsibility brings with it accountability. James asks the rhetorical question:

Who among you is wise and understanding [i.e., learned]? Let him show by his good behavior his deeds in the gentleness of wisdom (James 3:13).

"Will all the wise and learned teachers in the room please stand. Now, show your wisdom," says James, "by the quality of your life!" Wisdom, as I mentioned before (chapter 2) is used here in its Old Testament and Hebraic sense. Wisdom viewed in this way is tantamount to obedience. The truly wise man is one who has submitted his will to the law of God and is walking in obedience to it. Conversely, the fool is a rebel, not merely one who is untaught. Thus wisdom has nothing to do with intelligence or education. The issue is that of the heart rather than the mind. The word translated "understanding" does mean learned or expert. By juxtaposing these two terms (e.g., wise and learned) James reveals his understanding of the teaching task. The truly learned man is the wise man. The wise man is the Godlike man. Thus, when James calls for a teacher's credentials, he asks him to show his life. That life, not a diploma on the wall, is the true test of a teacher's qualifications.

THE MARKS OF TRUE WISDOM

There are specific characteristics which are marks of a mature man. Let me retranslate the last clause of verse 13 this way: "Let him show forth his works (remember 2:26) out of his good behavior and in a spirit of self-effacing obedience to God." The expression *gentleness of wisdom* actually means "a wisdom that doesn't insist on its own way or demand its own rights." That meaning is fitting in this context where jealousy and ambition seem to have become a way of life for teachers (v. 14). In contrast, the truly wise and learned man quietly and faithfully goes about his business of instructing others and leaves the results with God. He is similarly described by the Apostle Paul in this way:

> And the Lord's bond-servant must not be quarrelsome [or strive for mastery or recognition], but be kind to all, able to teach, patient when wronged, with gentleness correcting those who are in opposition (2 Tim. 2:24–25).

On the other hand, there are teachers who are striving against others and in their own interests: "But if you have bitter jealousy and selfish ambition in your heart, do not be arrogant and so lie against the truth" (James 3:14). Bitter jealousy is a sin against others. Selfish ambition is a sin against yourself. Instead of quietly relying on God for advancement, these teachers were promoting themselves and thus showing their pride and hypocrisy. They are arrogant, says James, and they are lying against the truth. No matter how orthodox they might be in their theology, if they are characterized by bitter jealousy and selfish ambition they are lying against the truth.

More Than Hypocrites

You might reason on this basis that if one does not live by the truth then he does not really know the truth. Or as someone has observed, "to know and not to do is not to know at all." That might be one way to look at the issue. James, however, actually takes us a step further. He reasons that to know and not to do is to teach contrary to the truth.

In other words, even though we know the truth, we are lying! We, in effect, teach lies about God. Thus the issue goes far beyond mere hyprocrisy. We are not merely hypocrites. We are heretics. That is the logical conclusion of James' teaching.

If one teaches about God by his life, then his students formulate their theology by observing his behavior. Their concept of God is developed out of the concept of God he displays. At this point the truth comes home. What are we teaching? What have others learned about God by observing our manner of life? James' argument is compelling and convicting. It ought to have force in our lives. None of us has any right to teach others if we are consciously and deliberately resisting the truth in any area of our lives. Our tongues and our behavior will ultimately betray us, and we will be found to be lying against the truth.

This is not to say, of course, that teachers have to be sinless. Who of us could qualify? James is saying, though, that we must judge any areas of unresolved rebellion in our lives and be willing to allow the Spirit of God to bring us into conformity to the Word of God. Anything less is heterodoxy (belief contrary to the truth). Truth in life is still the name of the game. That is why James demands that his audience show him their wisdom by living according to the truth.

If verses 13 and 14 are a demand for wisdom, then verses 15 through 18 are a description of it. In James' mind there are two kinds of wisdom: the wisdom from below (and here he uses the term *wisdom* ironically, vv. 15–16) and the wisdom from above (vv. 17–18):

This wisdom is not that which comes down from above, but is earthly, natural, demonic. For where jealousy and selfish ambition exist, there is disorder and every evil thing. But the wisdom from above is first pure, then peaceable, gentle, reasonable, full of mercy and good fruits, unwavering, without hypocrisy. And the seed whose fruit is righteousness is sown in peace by those who make peace (vv. 15–18).

The wisdom from below is earthly (e.g., secular) in its orientation. It is earthly because it has no higher reference point. It is limited by a finite, earth-bound perspective. In other words, it never rises higher than what man can do without God. It has no insight into man and his real needs. It can offer no counsel to touch the spirit of man. It can't save marriages or salvage lives. It has no power to accomplish anything lasting. Counselors of that sort abound. They may be sincere and thoroughly dedicated, but they have no real answers for man's desperate need. If, James argues, we do not back the truth with a living experience of it, we likewise will have nothing to say to our world.

Similarly, the wisdom from below is natural or soulish. We would describe it as sensual. It can gratify the senses, but not the spirit of man. And finally it is demonic. In James 2 we are told that the demons believe, but their belief does not modify their demonic character; they are demons to the end. Likewise, James argues, if we are not obedient to the truth we espouse, we have no more influence for good than the demons in hell.

Verse 16 tells us why this is so. Note that the verse begins with the conjunction *for* introducing an explanatory statement. Why is such wisdom the wisdom of this world? Because it ultimately produces turmoil and disorder. In chapter 4 James will further develop this idea. It is enough to say at this point that God's purpose is to bring peace to this troubled world. Satan's plan is to disrupt that peace. When we lie against the truth (and specifically he points out the dual sins of jealousy and ambition) we align our-

selves with the natural philosophy of secular modern man
and with the prince of this world. The result is chaos,
disorder and every vile practice.

But the wisdom from above is first pure (real, authentic),
then peaceful (restful), gentle (kind, yielding), reasonable
(nondefensive, compliant), full of mercy and good fruits
(for the weak and helpless). In addition it is unwavering
and without hypocrisy. "And the seed whose fruit is righteousness is sown in peace by those who make peace." In
other words, people who are truly wise will sow seeds
wherever they go that eventuate in a harvest of righteousness and peace. The products will be harmonious relation-
ships with God and man.

6

War and Peace

James 4:1–10

"What is the source of quarrels and conflicts among you?" (James 4:1*a*). That's a good question! How do you account for violence and war? The charter of the United Nations establishes the purpose of that body to be the discovery and eradication of the root causes of warfare. The conference at the Hague in the nineteenth century and the League of Nations had similar objectives. Yet we are today no closer to a solution than we were on the day that Cain slew Abel. The solution eludes us. The world today is filled with conflict and violence.

As I write these words, I'm thinking of yesterday's San Francisco Chronicle describing man's inhumanity to man in Ireland and South Africa. The conflict in the Middle East also rages on unabated. I'm certain that by the time you read these words there will be a fresh outbreak of violence on our war-torn globe.

And the situation is no better on an individual level. Home and family life is disintegrating at an alarming rate —indicating that the same turmoil and conflict exists between husband and wife, parents and children. What is the explanation for all this struggle and pain? Why can't we get along? Why do we rub each other the wrong way?

DESIRES THAT DIVIDE

James, having raised the question, answers (v. 1*b*): "Is not the source your *pleasures* that wage war in your members?" James goes immediately to the root cause. The problem lies within us. The source, he explains, is the pursuit of pleasure, and here a word of explanation is in order. The Greek term translated "pleasure" is the word *hedone* from which we get our English word *hedonism*. Hedonism is the philosophy that only what is pleasant or has pleasurable consequences is ultimately good. I recall a young philosopher friend of mine reading a Golden Book to one of my children some years ago. From the other room I heard him intone the words: "Let's all do the things we should. Good is fun and fun is good." "That," he said to Joshua very soberly, "is hedonism." Joshua, who was four years old at the time, couldn't appreciate his insight, but he was absolutely right. If you believe as an all-pervading principle of life that "fun is good" then you are indeed a hedonist. Some fun, of course, is not at all good and, therefore, most people, and certainly all genuine Christians, would reject hedonism as a way of life.

There is nothing wrong, of course, with pleasure. Life is filled with pleasurable things which God gave for our enjoyment. Nor is there anything intrinsically wrong with desiring or seeking pleasure. The pursuit of pain is not a Christian virtue. However, it is a sin to pursue pleasure at all costs—to make that aim the highest goal and to pursue it at the expense of someone else.

Let me illustrate from my own experience. I love to take showers! A long, hot shower is, I contend, a high and holy thing. However, it would be sin for me to spend an entire day standing in a shower stall or even to prolong that pleasurable experience unduly when someone else in the family needs to take a bath. My pursuit of pleasure must be regulated by my brother's needs—or in this case by that of my family. Their needs come first. It would be wrong for me to insist on my pleasure at their expense. Now this, I believe, is the force of James' argument. The *ruthless* pursuit of pleasure will inevitably bring me into a confrontation with my brother who likewise is pursuing a pleasurable end (perhaps we are even pursuing the same goal). Frustration will ensue and unless something or someone gives, the result will be quarreling and conflict.

Picture in your mind a hot, humid August day. You've been shopping for school clothes for the kids all day, rushing from one store to another; your feet are killing you. You've had it. But you have one more stop to make before you go home and collapse. Finally after circling the parking lot for the third time, you spot an empty space. Hooray, the only empty space in the lot! But just as you make the turn into the lane, another homemaker arrives simultaneously. Since it is an established law that two objects cannot normally occupy the same space at the same time, it is obvious that a crisis is imminent. One wonders how many people have been murdered or maimed for lesser reasons.

Or to take a more homely example: Husband arrives in the evening tired of talking to people all day and wants to retire behind the newspaper. Wife has talked to no one (over 5 years old) all day and has a marvelous store of anecdotes to share with husband. Both aims legitimate? But you can count on full-scale conflict (or at best a cold war) if both insist on pursuing those aims. The result will be frustration and inevitable conflict. The issue is really not any different whether we are talking about international or individual affairs. The pursuit of pleasure inevitably brings us into head-to-head conflict with others similarly inclined. The resultant thwarting of that aim leads to frustration and rage and eventually, if persisted in, results in quarreling and violence.

James elaborates in verse 2*a*:

> You lust [have strong passions] and do not have; so you commit murder. And you are envious and cannot obtain; so you fight and quarrel.

In other words, we fight and kill out of passion (an inordinate desire for anything) and jealousy (a desire for something that belongs to someone else). This warning may seem too strong. It does seem precipitous of James to leap to the conclusion that a frustrated desire could lead us to kill someone, but he is wise to so warn us. Any one of us, sufficiently frustrated, is capable of great violence or even murder. It is a fact that most homicides are not cold-blooded, premeditated murder, but rather crimes of passion, often deeply regretted after the fact. This principle which James enunciates is truth, and it ought to serve notice on the violent potential in all of us. One of our Supreme Court Justices recently said that the difference between the man on death row and the man on the street is not what he is but what he has done. Any one of us is capable of terrible acts of violence under sufficient provocation. James is right to blow the whistle on us. We are all potential killers. That is how far uncontrolled passion will drive us.

The principle now is clearly stated: Conflict is the result of the frustration of our drives for pleasure and satisfaction. We all participate in the problem. How can we be part of the solution?

JUST ASK

> You do not have because you do not ask. You ask and do not receive, because you ask with wrong motives, so that you may spend it on your pleasures (James 4:2*b*–3).

James' solution is profoundly simple—ask God. When your needs are not being met, ask God. When your desires for satisfaction are being frustrated, ask God. When in the pursuit of some pleasurable end you collide with a brother pursuing his pleasure and you are thwarted, ask God. Allow him to satisfy you with himself and his resources. He is the giver of every good thing (1:5, 17) and it delights his heart to give. Therefore ask.

I am reminded of the story of the man who, in a prayer meeting, launched into a lengthy, ponderous prayer, "Oh thou majestic God of the universe; who sitteth upon the circle of the earth, thou wind of God that bloweth where it listeth . . ." At which point an elderly lady behind him gave a tug on his coattail and said, "Just call him Father and ask him for something." That's James' point. Just ask him.

And ask him selflessly. Ask God to meet your needs in *his* way. It is possible to pressure the Father to achieve our own selfish ends. We want his power for our program. But that is not God's way. God has his own time and way for accomplishing his ends, and we dare not interfere. Delay is almost inevitably a part of the process. Also, God's ways are not our ways, and he frequently meets our needs in a most unexpected and unorthodox way. One mark of divine activity is that it is extraordinary and unconventional. God will surprise you almost every time. Therefore, we can't dictate the terms of our salvation or satisfaction. We have to be willing to let God do it in his own time and in his own way. Unfortunately, when God doesn't come through on schedule, our tendency is to cast about for another alternative—essentially an alternative to faith—rather than waiting on him for his solution.

I once heard a story about a man who was on the roof of his apartment building attempting to repair a television antenna. Unfortunately, in so doing, he lost his footing and fell over the side, saving himself at the last minute by grasping the edge of the rain gutter. "Help," he shouted, "Help, help, someone help me." Unfortunately no one heard him, whereupon, in desperation he looked up and shouted, "Is there anyone up there that can help me?" To his surprise, a voice answered "Yes, I will help you. Trust me. Let go." A moment's silence, then the man cried again, "Is there anyone *else* up there who can help me?" I think we all can identify!

MAKING GOD JEALOUS

Now remember, James is concerned in this section about a self-assertive spirit that pervades humanity—a spirit that drives us to hotly pursue our own pleasure without regard for God, man or beast. In fact, I believe the theme of self-assertion controls the wider context of James 4:1–5:11. We'll develop that thought in the following chapters. It is enough to say at this point that this independent spirit—this desire to have things when we want them and as we want them—is at the bottom of all strife. Proverbs states it most succinctly: "Through pride comes nothing but strife" (Prov. 13:10*a*). James indicts our acquisitive, grasping spirit as follows:

> You adulteresses, do you not know that friendship with the world is hostility toward God? Therefore whoever wishes to be a friend of the world makes himself an enemy of God. Or do you think that the Scripture speaks to no purpose: "He

jealously desires the spirit which He has made to dwell in us"?
(James 4:4–5).

Isn't it interesting how James describes us? When we
assert ourselves to achieve our own satisfaction we become
adulteresses. In other words, we are unfaithful to the Lord,
our loyal husband and provider. For example, I know of
few men who would appreciate their wives going to the
man next door to receive emotional support in a time of
stress. Most husbands want to provide that help themselves. They would be understandably upset if denied that
opportunity and replaced in that role by another man. God
likewise wants to supply our needs. We only have to ask.
When we try to satisfy ourselves from any other source,
we are behaving like unfaithful brides—adulteresses, to use
James' picturesque term.

Furthermore, we become a "friend of the world." That
is, we ally ourselves with the world and its ways of getting
things done. Self-assertiveness is the essence of worldliness.
Despite the current preoccupation with assertiveness
training, no one really has to train us to assert ourselves.
We are born with a penchant for it. Most of us excel at it.
And it is that spirit that produces strife and bitterness and
conflict as we have seen. On the other hand, God wants to
bring peace and effect reconciliation. As someone has said,
the activity of the world is centrifugal (a force that moves
things *outward*, away from the center). The activity of God
is centripetal (a force that brings things *inward*, toward the
center). Man scatters; God gathers.

So, if we side with the world in its moods and methods,
we are in conflict with God and thus constitute ourselves
the enemies of God. The so-called monsters of history, the
cruel tyrants and the oppressors of mankind are not the
only enemies of God. Anyone who has a policy of reckless
pursuit of pleasure (no matter how legitimate) is equally

in opposition to God. In other words, if I ignore my brothers' needs and linger in the shower or retreat into the evening paper to avoid communicating with the family, I have become the enemy of God. Do you see the issue? I am meeting my needs (for peace and quiet) in my own way and on my own terms instead of submitting to God and asking him to deal with them on his terms and in his way. And in failing to do so, I have become an enemy of God, a faithless bride. And that makes God jealous!

James quotes, "He jealously desires the spirit which he has made to dwell in us" (James 4:5). Even though the statement is introduced by the formula for an Old Testament quotation, you won't find that verse anywhere else in the Bible. James isn't thinking of a specific quotation but rather one predominant theme in the Old Testament—that of the jealousy of God for his people. Everywhere he is depicted as a loyal and loving husband who longs for purity and loyalty in his bride. The entire Bible forms the backdrop for James' statement. God wants to provide, and he is understandably incensed when he finds us in the arms of the world.

GRACE TO THE HUMBLE

But how does he respond to our infidelity? Not by rejection but by giving more of himself:

> But He gives a greater grace. Therefore it says, "God is opposed to the proud, but gives grace to the humble" (James 4:6).

Note that verse 6 is tied to verse 5 by the conjunction *but*. God's jealousy leads not to judgment, but greater generosity. He gives a greater grace (an undeserved gift). Greater than what? Greater than anything the world can provide. Or, as the hymnwriter put it:

He giveth more grace, when the burdens grow greater,
He sendeth more strength, when the labors increase,
To added affliction, He addeth His mercy,
To multiplied trials, His multiplied peace.

(Chorus)
His love has no limit,
His grace has no measure,
His power has no boundary known unto man,
For out of His infinite riches in Jesus,
He giveth and giveth and giveth again.
—Annie Johnson Flint

And in support of his contention that God wants to bestow grace on us, James quotes again the Old Testament, this time from a specific promise in Proverbs 3:34. God is unalterably opposed to those who don't want his help, but he gives without measure to the humble.

ATTAINING HUMILITY

Submit therefore to God. Resist the devil and he will flee from you. Draw near to God and He will draw near to you. Cleanse your hands, you sinners; and purify your hearts, you double-minded. Be miserable and mourn and weep: let your laughter be turned into mourning, and your joy to gloom. Humble yourselves in the presence of the Lord, and He will exalt you (James 4:7–10).

Now if you will look at the text before us you will notice that verses 7–10 are essentially a description of the humbling process that makes God's grace available to us. Note that the entire section is bracketed by the idea of humility (vv. 6 and 10). Furthermore, observe that these verses, introduced as they are by the conjunction *therefore*, represent the logical consequences of the truth in verse 6. Therefore, because God is opposed to the proud but gracious to the humble, what is one's logical response: First, we are to submit to God; that is, let God be God. Recall, as we saw in chapter one, that God has sovereignly chosen this frustrating circumstance for you. The little hands that beat on my bathroom door as I sing in the shower are really the hands of God. Alas!

There is a powerful parable in the Gospels (Matt. 20: 1–16) about a landowner who sent laborers into his field at various times of the day. Some went early and worked through the heat of the day; others went later. Some worked only one hour. But all were paid the same agreed-upon wage. Those who bore the brunt of the labor complained. The husbandman explained: "Do I not have the right to do as I please with my vineyard?" The lesson of the parable is clear. We must allow God to be God and submit to him, no matter how inconvenient or unjust it may seem to us.

Next, he says we are to resist the devil and he will flee from us. There is, I believe, a cause-and-effect relationship between the two commands in verse 7. When we submit to God, we are in fact resisting the devil. On the other hand, when we submit to the devil we are resisting God (as we know from verse 4). There are really only two options in life. We are either submitting to God or Satan. By submitting to one, we are in effect resisting the other.

It was apparently Satan's self-assertion that led to his downfall, and he is the one who holds the human race in bondage with that philosophy. He has successfully duped the world into believing in itself and asserting itself; and as James has warned us, it is that belief and assertion that lies at the bottom of all conflict. Therefore it is essential that by repudiating that lie, we resist the devil and submit to God.

Third, draw near to God and he will draw near to you.

Start laying hold of his resources. He is the one who sustains in any circumstance. It may not be his will to remove the inhibiting factors. You may be prevented from realizing your desires. And yet in the midst of that frustrating circumstance, he will draw near to you, he will give more grace. He will supply all that you need and minister to you richly. He will provide the strength and the patience to endure. If you draw near to God, he will draw near to you. You will find him faithful.

Fourth, "Cleanse your hands, you sinners; and purify your hearts, you double-minded." Deal with the actions (hands) and attitudes (hearts) that create these problems. Cleanse yourself from *all* defilement of the flesh. A thorough cleanup is in order.

Fifth, "Be miserable and mourn." In other words, take these faulty attitudes and actions seriously. Don't treat them lightly. An unjudged, self-assertive attitude or action can touch off the most devastating conflict, so don't blithely dismiss this exhortation. This is not merely good advice, a pleasant sentiment. We *must* let the Spirit of God deal with the attitudes and actions which cause conflict. The alternative is chaos.

Finally, by way of summary, James says, "Humble yourselves in the presence of the Lord, and He will exalt you" (v. 10).

Let him exalt you. Do not exalt yourself. In Philippians 2, Paul says of Jesus:

. . . who, although He existed in the form of God, did not regard equality with God a thing to be grasped, but emptied Himself, taking the form of a bond-servant, and being made in the likeness of men. And being found in appearance as a man, He humbled Himself by becoming obedient to the point of death, even death on a cross. Therefore also God highly exalted Him, and bestowed on Him the name which is above every name, that at the name of Jesus every knee should bow, of those who are in heaven, and on earth, and under the earth, and that every tongue should confess that Jesus Christ is Lord, to the glory of God the Father.

The Lord had to go to the place of death, and that is where we have to go. We have to be willing to take our most legitimate needs and desires and drives and ambitions and put them to death. Because Jesus was willing to die to himself, God exalted him and gave him the name which is above every name. The Father exalted him because he was willing to submit to the Father. And the Father will exalt us, if we are willing to humble ourselves under his hand. Perhaps James had Jesus' words in mind, "And whoever exalts himself shall be humbled; and whoever humbles himself shall be exalted" (Matt. 23:12).

In summary, then, the root cause of conflict is the ruthless, selfish pursuit of our own pleasure. The cure for conflict is a quiet rest in God who will supply our deepest needs and longings in his own time and in his own way. Just call him *Father* and ask him for something.

7

Playing God
and Other Perils

James 4:11–5:13

I have mentioned that chapters 4 and 5 are part of a continuing argument pertaining to the dangers of a self-assertive spirit. In chapter 4:1–10 we saw that it is the source of conflict and warfare. In the following paragraphs we will see it as the source of a critical spirit toward our brothers and sisters (4:11–12); and a presumptuous attitude toward our chosen vocations (4:13–17); a resentful heart toward those who oppress us (5:1–12); and a tendency to exploit our knowledge of God (5:13).

Judging a Brother

Do not speak against one another, brethren. He who speaks against a brother, or judges his brother, speaks against the law, and judges the law; but if you judge the law, you are not a doer of the law, but a judge of it. There is only one Lawgiver and Judge, the One who is able to save and to destroy; but who are you who judges your neighbor? (James 4:11–12).

The self-assertive spirit that causes conflict also makes us critical of one another. Jesus made that fact plain from the parable of the two men praying in the temple (Luke 18:9 f.). It was the self-righteous spirit of the Pharisee that made him contemptuous of his sinner-brother.

Verse 11 opens with a command. The reason for the command follows. The command is literally, "stop speaking against your brother"—evidently an ongoing practice, then as now. Nonredemptive criticism, sadly, is still with us. We all engage in it. At least I must plead guilty. It is a passion we can indulge in freely and without guilt because we have developed ways to disguise it. We are merely being "discerning." We are concerned about our brother and thus feel the need to "share" his weakness; what's worse, we enlist others to pray about it. But no matter how we mask it, it is still sin, and it is devastating! Therefore, James says, "Stop speaking against one another."

His explanation for this command is that when we do criticize a brother we are, in fact, playing God. We are sitting in judgment on the law (which God gave) and saying that we can, when necessary, rescind divine law. The law says, "Love your neighbor as yourself." That, as we have seen, is the quintessence of the law. When I choose to judge my brother harshly I am actually choosing to elevate myself above the law. I am, for the moment, repealing that law, James reasons, in order to indulge myself. I am now the judge of right and wrong—what is loving and what is not. I am now the measure of all things. I am interpreting the law instead of doing it. In short, I am playing God.

"Who do you think you are?" James continues (v. 12). "There is only one Lawgiver and Judge." There is only one who has divine prerogatives. Only he can save or destroy. Only God has infinite knowledge and power and, thus, can establish and maintain moral order. And he has not relinquished that right to anyone. How dare we, then, usurp his authority? Who do we think we are anyway? That is what James is saying. It strikes me as a very direct and profound approach to this matter of a judgmental spirit.

He is right, of course. In order to judge a brother justly I would have to know everything. I would have to know not only my brother's external circumstances, but also his inner thoughts and motives—an impossibility given my finite nature. I am most ungodlike in that respect. I never know what anyone is thinking. I'm not even sure of my own motives, come to think of it. How can I then presume to judge my brother's. And that, of course, is precisely James' point. Such judgment is presumptuous. Paul states the principle this way:

> Therefore do not go on passing judgment before the time, but wait until the Lord comes who will both bring to light the things hidden in the darkness and disclose the motives of men's hearts; and then each man's praise will come to him from God (1 Cor. 4:5).

He picks up James' point that such judgment is *presumptuous* (only God knows, and therefore can disclose the motives of men's hearts), but he adds another thought: Such judgment is also *premature*. God has fixed a time to judge the hearts of men. Any judgment now is "before the time." A third element in Paul's parallel treatment is that quite contrary to our expectations, each man will receive praise from God. We expect him him to get what he deserves (note we would never ask for that ourselves), but God deals in mercy and grace, and therefore, the outcome is praise. That's comforting when you think about it.

The real point, of course, is that we cannot judge a brother from our finite perspective. Any assessment of our brother's actions ought to be positive. After all, James says that God will praise him. What right have I to damn him?

I simply do not have enough information. If I did, I might construe his actions differently.

I have been told that once a group of young men decided to play a practical joke on a friend, a young bachelor executive who worked with them for an insurance firm in Dallas, Texas. It was the custom each Thanksgiving for the president of that firm to give free turkeys to all employees. The young friend had indicated his displeasure at the idea, since being a bachelor he had no idea what he would do with a whole turkey and, furthermore, had little desire to cook it. His friends, therefore, confiscated his turkey and replaced it with one made out of paper mâché, the only remains of the original bird being the neck and tail which protruded from the paper wrapping at the appropriate ends. The day before the holiday, the birds were handed out ceremoniously and our friend, unaware of the switch, tucked his bogus bird under his arm and caught the streetcar for home.

As he was sitting there, feeling a little self-conscious, a man seated himself on the bench next to him. Since the turkey was an obvious conversation piece, they soon were thus engaged. In the course of time the young man learned that his companion was without a job and had been down on his luck for some time. Therefore, he had dim prospects for a happy Thanksgiving. He was, in fact, on his way home with a few pounds of hamburger meat wrapped and tucked away in his coat pocket, and that would be the Thanksgiving meal for his family. Whereupon our friend had a brilliant idea. Why not swap? He had no use for the bird. Hamburger suited him fine. The man, of course, was delighted. Such generosity was overwhelming to him. So with a great sense of gratitude they made the exchange. Of course you can imagine the outcome, and the man's thoughts when he removed the wrappings from the turkey, his children crowding around wide-eyed with anticipation.

To keep the record straight, the young man, when he learned what his friends had done, looked for days for the man that he had unwittingly cheated, but unfortunately he was never found. The point, of course, is obvious. The poor defrauded man, from his vantage point, would never understand the young man's actions. To this day I'm sure that incident stands out in his mind as a classic example of man's inhumanity to man. Yet from the young man's point of view his motives were pure. The point for us, therefore, is to judge nothing before the time. We just don't have the necessary facts.

REDEMPTIVE JUDGMENT

To put things in balance, the Bible does speak of an act of judgment that is redemptive and should be carried out on our brothers' behalf. It is the judgment that Paul alludes to in Galatians 6:1:

> Brethren, even if a man is caught in any trespass, you who are spiritual, restore such a one in a spirit of gentleness; looking to yourself, lest you too be tempted.

And Jesus himself says in Matthew 18:15: "And if your brother sins, go and reprove him in private; if he listens to you, you have won your brother." That is not judgment with a view to condemnation, but rather one that is designed to save. It's a rescue operation! If we see a fellow believer violating a clearly revealed command of Scripture, we should call him to repentance in a spirit of love and humility. That's love in action! Redemptive judgment is based on actions (not motives) and violation of Scripture (not merely conscience) and is designed to restore and rebuild in a climate of acceptance and empathy—a far cry from the bitter criticism James describes here.

CHARTING YOUR COURSE

Now James moves to another area of life where we are inclined to play God—our commercial ventures:

> Come now, you who say, "Today or tomorrow, we shall go to such and such a city, and spend a year there and engage in business and make a profit." Yet you do not know what your life will be like tomorrow. You are just a vapor that appears for a little while and then vanishes away. Instead, you ought to say, "If the Lord wills, we shall live and also do this or that." But as it is, you boast in your arrogance; all such boasting is evil. Therefore, to one who knows the right thing to do, and does not do it, to him it is sin (James 4:13–17).

Evidently, even among these persecuted believers, merchants were plying their trades. After all, life must go on. There are mouths to feed and the wolf to be kept from the door. Planning and profitmaking are pursuits even the oppressed have to take into account. So it is not so startling to find these words addressed to this particular group. What is striking is that James suggests that such simple things as plans and profit can be sin. In fact, such activities are so much a part of the normal pursuits of life that it is strange indeed that James describes them as arrogant and boastful (v. 16) and therefore sinful (v. 17). Do you think of them in that way? I seldom do.

Let's look carefully at the passage. The sin of these believers lay not in the fact that they were engaging in work. Work, obviously, is not sinful. Work, like the family, existed before the fall. The fall merely made work labor. It didn't turn it into sin. In fact, the Bible clearly says that indolence is sin (2 Thess. 3:6–15). Therefore James cannot be condemning business ventures as such.

Nor is he condemning profit-making. Again, the profit motive, as such, is never condemned in Scripture. To be sure, profit-making at the expense of men, their personalities, our souls or our environment, *is* sin. But making a profit is not in itself anything to be spoken against. Nor is there anything inherently wrong with planning. Would that more of us did more of it! Many times, I'm sure you have said in effect what James' hypothetical merchant says, "Today or tomorrow, we shall go to such and such a city and spend a year there and engage in business there." Business trips are a necessary though disagreeable part of most occupations. It is frequently the difference between survival and failure in one's business. Planning for such ventures, therefore, is essential. No, James is not forbidding planning or profit-making. What he is condemning is the attitude that often underlies those activities: "Who needs God? I can do it all by myself." That's the heart of the matter. Again, we are planning apart from God. Once more we are playing God. We act as though we alone can control our destiny. And as James points out, that simply isn't true.

We do not know what our life will be like tomorrow. We cannot predict the future; that is God's prerogative. We have remarkable hindsight, but very poor ability to anticipate with any degree of reliability what will occur tomorrow. What's more, even if we knew what the future held, we would be impotent to do anything about it. How many "chance" happenings irrevocably alter a man's life? When you think back on your life it becomes apparent that all of us are in the grip of inexorable forces. We think we are free to choose, yet how many of us have had our lives radically changed by events that are completely beyond our control?

Several years ago, I was involved in an automobile accident in which the passenger in my car was killed. After the tragic event I recalled that he had almost missed our appointment. He had forgotten our luncheon date and was going elsewhere to eat. It was mere "chance" that I arrived at the front door of his office at the precise instant that he left with another friend. Had I arrived a moment or two later I would have missed him completely. Was it likewise only chance that my Volkswagen and a moving van arrived at the same intersection simultaneously? Was it chance that my seat belt was fastened and his was not?

As I put that series of terrifying events together I saw again the truth James is stressing. We are never in control of our lives. It is arrogance to assume that we are and plan accordingly. We should rather say, "If the Lord wills, we shall do this or that." To think otherwise is sheer pride and presumption.

The thought, "Lord willing," is not, of course, merely an aphorism used to sanctify one's plans. James intends it to be a heartfelt conviction. It is something we ought to feel inwardly, not necessarily repeat verbally. In fact, it need never be said at all, but it should be part of the warp and woof of our thinking. We may plan and propose, but God always has the last word. As ancient wisdom stated it, "Many are the plans in the mind of a man; but it is the purposes of the Lord that are established." And we had better believe it. To believe otherwise is sin.

Now James turns to his third and final point. Our tendency to play God is revealed by our attitude toward those who oppress us.

Come now, you rich, weep and howl for your miseries which are coming upon you. Your riches have rotted and your garments have become moth-eaten. Your gold and your silver have rusted; and their rust will be a witness against you and will consume your flesh like fire. It is in the Last Days that you have stored up your treasure! Behold, the pay of the laborers who mowed your fields, and which has been withheld by you, cries out against you; and the outcry of those who did the harvesting has reached the ears of the Lord of Sabaoth. You have lived luxuriously on the earth and led a life of wanton pleasure; you have fattened your hearts in a day of slaughter. You have condemned and put to death the righteous man; he does not resist you. Be patient, therefore, brethren, until the coming of the Lord. Behold, the farmer waits for the precious produce of the soil, being patient about it, until it gets the early and late rains. You too be patient; strengthen your hearts, for the coming of the Lord is at hand. Do not complain, brethren, against one another, that you yourselves may not be judged; behold, the Judge is standing right at the door. As an example, brethren, of suffering and patience, take the prophets who spoke in the name of the Lord. Behold, we count those blessed who endured. You have heard of the endurance of Job and have seen the outcome of the Lord's dealings, that the Lord is full of compassion and is merciful (James 5:1–11).

First, some general observations about this passage. Remember that the people to whom this letter was addressed were a suffering people. They were being cruelly oppressed by both their Jewish brethren and by the Gentile community. They were a minority group within a minority group. So this is not mere theory. James is confronting reality.

Second, you will note that James apparently addresses both groups in this section: the oppressors (5:1–6) and the oppressed (5:7–11). You will also notice that the commands in the second division (5:7–11) are in logical sequence with what he says to the oppressors ("Be patient, therefore . . ."). Now let's turn to the passage itself.

THE CONDEMNATION OF THE RICH

Wealth and misery often go hand in hand. They don't have to, but they frequently do. Wealth, per se, does not cause misery, but ill-gotten wealth almost always does. In the context here James is clearly speaking to people who have acquired wealth by taking advantage of others. It is for that reason alone that misery is coming on them. The miseries associated with their ill-gotten riches may not come during their lifetime, but it is a fact that they will come. James says, "Your riches *have rotted* and your garments *have become moth-eaten.* Your gold and silver *have rusted* . . ." James puts these verbs all in the past tense and thus implies that these corrupting effects are as good as accomplished.

Furthermore, note that he says their gold and silver have *rusted.* Everyone knows that gold and silver do not rust, but James uses this striking language to emphasize the impermanent value of earthly riches in the ultimate scheme of things. That which men place their highest value on to the extent of squashing anyone who gets in their way has no value at all when it comes to God's final judgment of men's lives. Rust is a symbol of the corruption of values that puts gold and silver above the concerns of people. (In other words, they know the price of gold but not its value.) That rust, James says, "will be a witness against you and will consume your flesh like fire." He says, "You may think you are amassing gold and silver for your own benefit, but what you're really doing is storing up a vast 'treasure' of rust, which will ultimately be your destruction! You have the attitude that this life on earth is all there is, but you are wrong. Life is eternal, and everything you do has eternal significance. Everyone dies, physically, but everyone is also raised—either to eternal life in the glorious presence of Jesus Christ or to eternal darkness. There, Jesus said, will be wailing and gnashing of teeth. It is in the Last Days that you have stored up your treasure!"

FATTENED FOR SLAUGHTER

This brings us to James' most telling point. Oppression moves God to anger and action. He will not stand by and allow exploitation to go on forever. God hears, and God knows. God hears the cries of the oppressed workers. Even their withheld wages are an eloquent witness to the injustice of their oppressors. And this outrage has reached the ears of the Lord of Sabaoth. Here James reaches into their Old Testament memories for a particularly relevant title for God. The Lord of Sabaoth (or Hosts) was the Lord of heavenly hosts, angelic hosts, the armies of the world and more particularly, the Captain of the hosts of Israel. He is, in fact, the Commander-in-chief of the entire universe. It is this sovereign Lord who is stirred to holy outrage by the plight of the oppressed. He is coming to set things right. Oh, not right off, you understand. He is not trying now to run the world right. He could if he so chose, but right now he is letting men have their day. He is allowing them to do as they please and reap the consequences of their choices. But he knows, and one day he will have his day. That's what the prophets meant when they referred to that event as the Day of the Lord. Man has his day now, but God will yet have his day. And that will be the *last* day. Then everything will be set right. Every injustice rectified, every wrong redressed.

> Though the mills of God grind slowly,
>   yet they grind exceeding small;
> Though with patience he stands waiting,
>   with exactness grinds He all.
> —Friedrich Von Logau

James' bold metaphor stirs my memory. "You have fattened your heart in a day of slaughter." I recall an era in my life when I lived in Texas. I was in a 4H Club and applied to the county farm agent for a pig to raise. Eventually I was given one, and then, as the arrangement stipulated, allowed to keep all of her litter except one, which was returned to the county. We decided in due course that we

would butcher one pig ourselves for meat and conse-
quently began to fatten that pig for slaughter. I can remember with what grim determination I encouraged that pig
to eat. While I gleefully stimulated her appetite with savory
scrap, I anticipated the satisfaction of my own. She was
indeed fattening herself for the day of slaughter. Likewise,
James warns the wealthy oppressors that they are hasten-
ing the day of their judgment by their voracious appetites.
The Lord of Hosts is coming.

It's worth noting one grisly fulfillment of James' predic-
tion. Some twenty-five or thirty years later when the Roman General Titus captured the city of Jerusalem, after a
lengthy siege he tortured the obese citizens of the city to
get possession of their wealth. It was obvious they had
access to resources the starving populace did not have!

He further accuses them of condemning and putting to
death the righteous man. Some think James is accusing the
wealthy of putting Jesus, the righteous man, to death. I
think not. I believe, rather, that James is introducing an
axiom into their thinking. He is saying in effect that regard-
less of the actions taken against a righteous man, he does
not resist. This may be stated as a principle: righteous men
do not resist their oppressors. As Jesus was mute before his
accusers and nondefensive throughout his entire trial and
crucifixion, so righteous men do not resist, no matter how
much injustice they may encounter.

Now we need to make a counterstatement to put things
in balance. The Bible never approves passivity when *others'*
rights are at stake. There may be occasions when you must
defend the rights of others. In fact, there are times when
to withhold defense would be outrageous. Who, for instance, would stand by while a child was being cruelly
beaten? God gets angry. Jesus was enraged by the activities
of the moneychangers who were defrauding his people and
defiling his Father's house. There is something wrong with

an individual who has no capacity for anger when others are cheated and defrauded. When another's rights are violated, it ought to make us angry. There is no love if there is no anger. However, James and the rest of the writers of Scripture are very clear. Righteous men do not retaliate when *their* rights are violated. James states it axiomatically: he (the righteous man) does not resist (cp. Matt. 5:39).

ENCOURAGEMENT TO THE OPPRESSED

What action, then, can the righteous take? "Be patient, therefore, . . . until the coming of the Lord." Don't resist. Wait for the Lord to set things right. Anything short of patience is presumption. Do you see him returning to his theme again? Don't take things into your hands. Don't rise up and throw off the yoke of oppression. Defend your brother if you will, but don't defend yourself. Let the Lord be your defense. Be patient; have a long fuse. Be calm and restful, like the farmer that waits for the harvest. This illustration is fitting, with its emphasis on awaiting due process. The farmer plants the seed and then awaits the inevitable process of growth. He doesn't plant one day and despair the next because the crop doesn't appear. Nor should we despair because the Lord does not appear. He is coming as certainly as the harvest. The farmer merely has to wait and his efforts will be rewarded. Your reward is likewise determined; wait, be patient, and in due time the Lord will come to set all things right.

I once heard the most delightful story of an elderly couple who had served with distinction as missionaries in Africa. Now after more than fifty years of faithful but unheralded ministry, they were returning home to retire. To their delight they were booked on a flight with the Beatles, the British singing group, who at that time were at the pinnacle of their popularity here in the States. Their enjoyment was short-lived however. When they arrived in

New York City they were met by a mob of teenagers there to greet the Beatles and found it difficult to get through the crowd to the waiting room. After being pushed and almost trampled for some minutes they made their way to the reception area only to find much to their dismay that there was no one to greet them. Through some oversight the mission board had failed to send a welcoming party. The old gentleman was particularly annoyed, and even though they found a taxi and soon got out of the airport, he was terribly distressed by what seemed to him to be a gross breach of etiquette.

Eventually, they found the way to their apartment and with difficulty moved their bags into the home where they planned to live out the rest of their retirement. Again, their mission board inadvertently had made no arrangements for assistance. This, it seemed, was the last straw for the elderly gentleman. "What gratitude," he fumed. "The Beatles arrive, and the entire city turns out. We come home after fifty years of service, and there is no one to greet us." "Not true," returned his wife. "You see, we're just not home yet." And that, of course, was the right perspective on things. That's the eternal perspective. We should not expect people to treat us justly in this life. They probably won't. The churches in Asia Minor awarded the Apostle Paul for thirty-five years of faithful service by rejecting him (2 Tim. 1:15). Nero rewarded him by cutting off his head. The "Well done, good and faithful servant" comes when we see the Lord. He will set all things right. Therefore, be patient until that day.

Second, "strengthen your hearts" (literally, "prop up your hearts"). Strengthen them in the knowledge that the Lord is at hand. He is, in fact, standing right at the door (v. 9). He is coming soon! Therefore, strengthen your heart with this knowledge.

His proximity raises a third concern. Because he is right

at hand, James writes, "stop complaining against one another." Or as *The New English Bible* translates this verse, "Do
not blame your troubles on one another, or you will fall
under judgement . . ." (James 5:9). So don't blame your
problems on your brother (which we tend to do when the
real source of our misfortune is inaccessible to us). Don't
complain and take out your bitterness on others—your
spouse and children. Instead take heart in the resources of
the Lord of Hosts and the example of the prophets. They,
like James' readers, were not immune to suffering. They
were oppressed as few men in history have been.

But don't focus on their suffering, James argues. Look
instead at the Lord's dealings with them. Look at Job, for
example. What do you learn from Job's example of quiet
dependence and patience through his suffering? You learn,
according to James, that the Lord is full of compassion and
mercy. James' conclusion ("that the Lord is full of compassion and is merciful") is actually a quotation from the Old
Testament, probably a composite quote in which James
links together two verses from different parts of the Old
Testament (Exod. 34:6; Ps. 103:8). His point is that men
who suffer experience a unique sense of the pity and sym-
pathy of God. They do not feel that they are alone. They
believe that God is in it with them just as he walked with
the three Hebrew children through the fiery furnace (Dan.
3:25).

You might reason from James' reference to Job that he
is pointing to the restoration of Job's fortunes. And it is
difficult indeed to integrate that point of view with all that
we know about the Lord's dealings with us. He does not
always restore our fortunes to us—at least not in our lifetime. Certainly he did not restore Jeremiah to good fortune.
As far as we know, one of his own countrymen in Egypt
stoned him to death. No, it is not the earthly outcome
James has in mind. Actually the word translated "out-

come" is the word *end* or *ultimate purpose*. God had a greater purpose than to merely make Job once more healthy, wealthy and wise. His ultimate purpose was to instruct Job about his character. And Job received that instruction, as we know from his comments at the end of the book. Job, among other things, learned that the Lord is both sympathetic and full of pity. In other words, he cares! It matters to him about us.

Therefore, in those depressing times, when we are unjustly and unfairly treated (by employers, family, or friends), we can patiently wait for God to redress all wrongs and, meanwhile, rest in the knowledge that he knows and cares about us. And what's more, we can count ourselves blessed (5:11) along with those great prophets of old who suffered and endured. The result is peace. Seeds of peace are sown in our heart and in others with a resultant great harvest of peace.

PROHIBITION AGAINST SWEARING

And finally, James says:

> But above all, my brethren, do not swear, either by heaven or by earth or with any other oath; but let your yes be yes, and your no, no; so that you may not fall under judgment (James 5:12).

You may know that this verse is merely a shortened form of Jesus' command in Matthew 5:33–37. Both have in mind the same prohibition. Here James is not concerned with blasphemy or lewd talk, though he well might have been. In this particular section he is referring rather to the widespread practice of affirming a promise or declaration by means of an oath. In other words, it is a solemn oath that James has in mind. What is prohibited is evoking an oath to strengthen a declaration, swearing by heaven or by God or, as Jesus said (Matt. 5:35, 36), by Jerusalem or by the hair of your head or chin.

It does seem strange that James would forbid what appears to be merely an innocent and harmless use of an oath. Yet there evidently was a practice in James' day that made this prohibition necessary. It appears that it had become common practice to link God's name with a declaration of intent. In some way they believed that this practice would bind God to act on their behalf. If they vowed to do a thing and then evoked the name of God as their surety, then God would be obligated to do what they had promised. We have to speculate somewhat, because we just do not know precisely how this practice originated. However, my feeling is that it grew out of a distortion of the commands in the Torah governing oaths (Lev. 19:12; Num. 30:2; Deut. 23:21). It was a serious thing under the law to violate an oath. If one took such an oath he was obligated to fulfill it. Human nature being what it is, most men failed to follow through. Thus both the man who took the oath and the Lord whose name was evoked in the oath fell into dishonor. Since the honor of God's name was at stake, therefore, the law made oath-taking a serious matter not to be lightly undertaken.

The Jews in a later period, however, circumvented that purpose of the law by declaring that an oath once taken in the name of the Lord (or by anything associated with his worship) obligated God to fulfill the oath. You can see how they were reasoning. God's name is at stake in this oath. Therefore, if I take an oath, he must act to fulfill it. To put it bluntly, they were blackmailing God. They had no intention of determining God's will and asking for it. They were rather asserting their own will and insisting that God prosper it. It is that practice which James condemns and prohibits.

That being the case, you can readily see how this command fits into the context. This is merely another way of

playing God. We determine what action we will take and
what the result of that action will be and then insist that
God endorse and bless those plans. And in so acting, we
engage again in the same sort of self-assertive activity James
has been speaking against throughout this section of his
book. And so James concludes by insisting once more that
we judge such attitudes, or we will fall under God's judgment. We do not fall into "condemnation" as some transla-
tions have it. This is not a final judgment; it is the judgment
which all sons of God receive from their Heavenly Father
(Heb. 12:5–11). If we do not chasten ourselves, then the
Father will! Therefore, James says, judge yourself that you
be not judged.

This practice which James forbids is so contrary to our
experience that it is difficult to see any current application.
Few of us really feel that we bind God with our oaths. In
fact, oath-taking as such (except in a court of law) is foreign
to us. Most of the oaths we take ("I swear I will do it," etc.)
are fairly trivial and do not particularly fall under this
prohibition. Certainly oath-taking in a court of law does
not. The solemn oath that we take in court is merely a way
of insuring the truthfulness of one's word and is a conces-
sion to secular society and their awareness that fallen man
is prone to distortion and deceit. Such an oath makes it less
likely that a witness will lie. Therefore, it certainly doesn't
fall under the judgment of which James speaks.

James has something else in mind. It is, as we have seen,
the tendency that we all have to act as though we are
independent, self-sufficient beings. In this specific case it
is our tendency to make cavalier, high-handed decisions
without consulting God or waiting for his counsel. It is this
impertinence that keeps us from experiencing the "outcome of the Lord's dealings" (v. 11). When actually or seem-
ingly oppressed we tend to make rash and presumptuous
decisions based on what we believe to be our immediate

needs. And then we expect, as a matter of course, that God will bail us out or bring us through. In either case we are, in fact, doing what James interdicts. Though we have not actually stated our intention in the form of a formal oath, we have nevertheless acted in such a way that we believe God is now obligated to act on our behalf. It is merely another attempt on our part to usurp God's power for our program. Instead of waiting and relying on God to act in his own time and in his own way, we try to force God into action, blackmail him into doing something now and doing it our way. And James says, "Above all" resist such audacity. Don't try to coerce God into acting in any particular way. Let God be God!

Looking back over this lengthy section we can draw one conclusion. Life has its perils. There are brothers whose actions we find difficult to understand. There are business and vocational decisions that are beyond our ken. There are acts of injustice and cruelty that will anger and frustrate us. In all of these matters we are tempted to dictate the terms of our deliverance, rather than submit to God's will. Our response in each case ought to be "Not my will but yours be done." Any other response requires that we assert ourselves and play God. And of all the perils in life, that is the most hazardous. We do it at our own risk.

8

Praying and Caring

James 5:13–20

Our three sons, whom I regard as accidents going somewhere to happen, have taught me that life is made up of weal and woe. I have lost track of the number of runs to the hospital for x-rays and stitches, assorted pills and repairs. One never knows what a day will bring. At least life never gets dull for parents. Also, as a pastor, I've become accustomed to the vicissitudes of life. Life is an alternation of good and bad, health and sickness, prosperity and adversity. Change is constant; the status is never quo. As we used to say in Texas, "If you don't like the weather, just wait a minute."

In addition to our changing circumstances there are our changing moods. Often they have nothing to do with the outward events of our lives. For no apparent reason we may awaken with the blahs. Everything, for some unexplainable reason, looks bleak and gray. Other times, even in periods of severe pressure, we are chipper and optimistic. As the old spiritual has it, "Sometimes I'm up; sometimes I'm down." You never know what a day will bring or how you will feel about it. Our circumstances and our attitudes are in a constant state of flux. As James has noted before, "You do not know what your life will be like tomorrow" (James 4:14). Change and fluctuations of fortune are one of the hard facts of life. Therefore, we need one fixed point around which the ebb and flow of life can be ordered, something to keep us steady through the vicissitudes of life. And that James gives: "Is anyone among you suffering? Let him pray. Is anyone cheerful? Let him sing praises" (James 5:13).

Is anyone suffering? Are you beat? (The Greek word for *suffering* in verse 13 actually means suffering cruels blows from without.) Then pray. Are you cheerful? Full of vim, vigor and vitality? Then pray, sing praises. Praises, after all, are merely another form of prayer. In any and all circumstances, writes James, pray. In other words, relate everything to God. He is in everything, behind every circumstance, present in every event.

THE MYSTERY OF PRAYER

I recall a plaque over my mother's desk that said, "Prayer changes things." That's true; prayer does produce change. As James points out in this chapter (v. 16), the effective prayer of a righteous man can accomplish much (literally, "wins out" or "prevails"). When we pray, things happen! God promises it, and our experience confirms it. Yet we must know that God (simply because he is God) is not swayed by our entreaties. He can't be influenced to act in a way contrary to what he has already purposed. Prayer, or so I believe, has no persuasive effect on God.

What then is prayer? Prayer is a great mystery. (I'm not thinking here of a biblical "mystery," i.e., a truth revealed by God that we would not otherwise know.) We are simply not told how prayer works. There is, however, at least a partial explanation in Scripture. There is even a suggestion in the passage before us. Note the illustration of Elijah in verses 17 and 18. We are told that Elijah prayed and it did not rain for three and a half years. Again, we are told that he prayed and it rained. Surely this is an example of vigorous intercessory prayer. Yet when you read the account in 1 Kings 17 and 18, you will find only one rather obscure reference to Elijah at prayer. As a matter of plain fact, Elijah's declaration to Ahab that it would "neither dew nor rain these years" is based on the Lord's *word* which had come to him (1 Kings 17:1). Additionally we are told that before Elijah prayed for the drought to be broken (18:42), he was *told* that it would be broken (18:1). In other words, he merely asked God to do what God had already said he would do! That, it seems, is always the characteristic of effective prayer. It is asking in line with God's purposes and promises. Paul, I believe, is stating the same principle another way in Romans 8:26, 27:

> And in the same way the Spirit also helps our weakness; for we do not know how to pray as we should, but the Spirit Himself intercedes for us with groanings too deep for words; and He who searches the hearts knows what the mind of the Spirit is, because He intercedes for the saints according to the will of God.

Paul states what we all feel. We simply do not know how to pray. Certainly if we don't feel that way, we should. Who of us knows enough to pray in such a way that God's purposes are accomplished? What audacity, for instance, to pray for a three-year drought as Elijah did? How could I know what effect that would have on the economy of the land of Canaan, the entire Near East or, for that matter, the whole world? Who could assess the environmental impact of that prayer? Any information that I might have would be short-range and mostly related to my personal needs. Therefore, if I'm honest, I must admit I do not know how to pray. However, writes Paul, the Spirit himself who knows the mind of God intercedes for us according to the will of God. Paul's point, I believe, is that it is futile to fill the air with cries and pleas when we are suffering (for that is the context here as well) because we do not know what to ask for. The Spirit helps us in our weakness, however, by praying for us, and *we thus are led to pray as he prays.* Prayer, then, is mostly listening. Prayer is finding God's will and asking for it. That will is revealed through the internal witness of the spirit of God to the written Word of God.

Prayer Changes Us

It works out in practice in this way, or so I believe. Suffering ought to cause us to wait on God. In time, as we submit to his will and accept our condition as his plan for us, he will reveal a promise or principle in his word. It may come from our own reading of scripture or the counsel of another or the recollection of some forgotten truth. But it will be relevant to our situation and will become the basis of renewed prayer. Often there is a great sense of boldness that accompanies such prayer. That is what the apostles describe as praying "in the spirit" (Eph. 6:18). That is authentic prayer! I do fully expect to see all such prayers answered, because they are firmly based on the faithfulness of God. He is the God who cannot lie (Titus 1:2). Therefore, what he promises, he performs. In time or in eternity all will be realized; of that I am sure.

Now do you see what has happened? God enlists us in the process of fulfilling his will. In other words, we by prayer share with him in what he has purposed to do in the world. Prayer thus is not our way of aligning God with our program, but his way of aligning us with his. Prayer works *on* you as well as *for* you. Prayer changes *you.* It relates you to what God is doing, as well as relating God to all elements of your life. It makes you a partner with God in his program to bring salvation to this earth. In short, it "can accomplish much." It can and may change the outward affairs of your life. It will always, if rightly used, change your attitude toward those circumstances. You will begin to see things from God's viewpoint and, having thus viewed them, will begin to agree with God that they are right and proper for you. Therefore, you can stop resisting and start resting in them. Prayer, thus, has changed you. This is, at least for me, a most satisfying explanation of the necessity for prayer. Therefore, James writes, pray about everything. If you are suffering—pray. If you are cheerful—pray. That's God's way of getting into every aspect of your experience.

James picks up the theme of prayer again in verses 14 and 15. But in this instance he has in mind a particular aspect of prayer:

> Is anyone among you sick? Let him call for the elders of the church, and let them pray over him, anointing him with oil in the name of the Lord; and the prayer offered in faith will restore the one who is sick, and the Lord will raise him up, and if he has committed sins, they will be forgiven him (James 5:14–15).

This passage is admittedly difficult and has been interpreted in various ways. It is this passage from which the Roman Catholic church derives its Sacrament of Extreme Unction, termed *extreme* because it is administered when the patient is *in extremis* or at the point of death. According to Roman Catholic theology, the last rites performed by the priest prepare the soul of man to enter into death. Accordingly the sign of anointing and prayer symbolize the grace given to man upon faith and repentance to produce strength of soul to face death. The emphasis in Roman

Catholic theology, then, is more on preparation for death than for life. It seems to me, however, that James' stress lies elsewhere. His emphasis is that this action, taken in faith, will restore a brother to *life*.

Others have assigned this passage to an early period of church history when healings authenticated the apostolic message (Heb. 1:4). It was legitimate for that hour and the particular needs of the church at that time, but has no relevance to our century. Thus they believe the passage has no meaning for us today. I believe, however, that this passage is spoken for our day as well. We must, therefore, take it literally and seriously. Because this passage is largely ignored today, this practice is absent from our churches. And I believe by so handling it we have weakened the ministry of the Word.

Let's make some observations. First note that this passage has something to do with the relationship of sickness and prayer. The prayer here specifically has to do with prayer for an *ailing* brother—primarily one who is physically sick. The term translated *sick* in verse 14 means "helpless or weak." In other words, this is an especially debilitating illness. The brother or sister is severely afflicted. The second term, translated *sick* in verse 15, actually means "weary." That is, the sufferer has grown weary because of the long duration of the illness. We can conclude, therefore, that James is not talking about minor ailments, but severe long-term disorders with accompanying physical pain and emotional discomfort; the victim is gravely ill.

Sɪᴄᴋɴᴇss ᴀɴᴅ Sɪɴ

Second, the sickness is related to sin. In one sense, of course, all sickness is related to sin. Sin, in general, causes sickness in general. The entrance of sin into the world through Adam brought about degeneracy and death. Our partnership with Adam means that we all get diseased and eventually die. So in that general sense, all such sickness is the result of sin.

Not all physical disorder, however, is the direct result of one's sinful acts. Jesus made that very clear when the disciples asked him, "Rabbi, who sinned, this man or his parents, that he should be born blind?" Jesus answered, "It was neither that this man sinned, nor his parents; but it was in order that the works of God might be displayed in him" (John 9:2–3). In other words, the pitiful plight of the blind man was not because the man himself sinned. There was no direct cause-and-effect relationship between this man's sin and his affliction. In his case it was permitted in order to display God's works in the man, specifically by giving him his sight and thus authenticating the work of God's Son (John 9:4). Other passages likewise indicate that not all calamity and sickness is the direct result of one's sin (cf. Luke 13:1–5). However, a substantial number of verses do indicate that sin can make one sick, even to death (Mark 2:5; 1 Cor. 30; Deut. 28:22, 27; John 5:14; 1 John 5:16, 17). And this seems to be the intent of James' words here. He is referring specifically to a sickness caused by sin.

You'll note that James says in verse 15, "And if he has committed sins, they will be forgiven him." In English all conditional clauses have one force. They convey a true contingency. In Greek, however, there are a number of ways to state a condition. In this particular case James uses a phrase that actually suggests a high degree of probability. It is not certain that he has committed sin. However, it is *most* probable. At least that is the way James views the situation before him.

In addition you should know that the verb in verse 15 translated "committed sins" suggests an action in the past with continuing results. In other words, they are sins that were committed in the past and are still exercising control over the individual. He is the victim of his sin. And there is only one class of sin that can victimize a Christian—un-judged, unconfessed sins. I believe, then, that these are not isolated sinful acts—sins which one may inadvertently or even deliberately fall into and then quickly judge. They are rather sins *persisted in*. That is, they are areas of rebellion which the individual in question has allowed to go un-judged. This is sinning with a high hand—deliberate, con-scious, long-term rebellion against some known command of God. And it is a well-established biblical fact that sin of that nature may produce weakness, sickness and even death (1 Cor. 11:30).

OPEN CONFESSION

Perhaps the strongest indication of James' intent is verse 16: "Therefore, confess your sins to one another, and pray for one another, so that you may be healed." The conjunc-tion *therefore* marks this sentence as a conclusion to what has preceded it. The argument, I believe, goes like this: Sin persisted in will make you sick and eventually kill you. *Therefore*, confess your sins to one another so you may be healed. (The verb suggests a state of being—a healed or healthy condition.) More about this verse later. My concern in introducing it at this point is to show that James' solu-tion to the sin that leads to death is open confession of that sin. He is directing us to deal with sin before it does us in! He is exhorting us to share our struggle with a brother and pray for one another that we may be healed as a condition of life, a state of being.

You can see, therefore, that this verse would have little significance in this context unless James is speaking about the dire effects of sin in one's life. Because sin will destroy us, James reasons, we must do something about sin. Call for help from a stronger member. There are some sins which can spring up quickly and with which we cannot cope. Some habits, likewise, are almost impossible to eradi-

cate. That's why we need the Body. In such cases, James
argues, confess your sins to one another and pray for one
another that you may be healed. Then, by way of reminder,
he underscores the radical effects of believing prayer. If
prayer can alter the forces of nature, it can most certainly
change us. James' entire argument hinges on the idea that
prayer will release one from sin which will in turn result
in health and a state of well-being. To violate this principle
may result in weakness, sin, and an untimely death.

These observations, then, have led me to believe that
James is here referring to sickness and suffering that is the
direct result of rebellion. This is sin that leads to death.
This is the sin that John says we should not beg God to
cure (1 John 5:16). That is, we should not plead with God
to merely terminate the illness because the real source of
the malady is deeply entrenched sin. If he healed in that
situation, he would merely be treating symptoms. The
man's need is fundamentally spiritual rather than physical.
In this case the only cure is genuine repentance and the
concerted ministry of the entire Body of Christ. The
confession of the ailing member and the intercession of a
believing Body will then result in wholeness of spirit and
body.

THE ONE-TWO PUNCH

Notice that James suggests two stages. Confession of sin
to one another keeps the body healthy spiritually and
physically (James 5:16). That is what James means when
he says, "Confess your sins to one another." The terminology suggests confessing to someone of the same kind,
a much needed reminder that we are all subject to failure.
We all need the support of the Body in our fight against
sin. The term *confession* implies frankness and openness
about our sins. It means essentially to agree with God about
the sin—to call it what it is and not rationalize it or justify

it. Name it and ask for help. Then the stronger member is to pray for us that we may be strengthened to resist the sin and thus delivered from it and its damaging effects. In such a case, James insists, we will continue in a state of good health.

If, however, we have allowed the sin to so control us that it has led to sickness, then we may, even in that advanced state, call for the elders of the church who will then, like any other member of the Body, and in fact representing that Body, pray for us that we may be healed. The result of such a prayer will be restoration and forgiveness (James 5:14, 15). Note that the ailing man takes the initiative. *He* calls for the elders (v. 14). They come in response to his call. The elders, in this case, because they are the leadership in a local assembly, represent that local group. That is, they come in place of the entire church. They represent the Body of Christ on a rescue mission! Thus, in effect, the whole Body ministers to the need of the ailing member.

This is a vivid analogy to the way in which our human body functions. If one part of our body is ailing, it cries out for help. Every other member comes to its aid. All the resources of our body are brought to bear on the infirmity of the weaker member. In this way the entire body takes on this weakness. The weak member takes on the strength of the whole organism. Thus the body ministers to itself. It is a fact that physicians cannot heal, but the body will heal itself if given the opportunity. All any physician can do is assist the body in its internal affairs. Given half a chance, our bodies will correct almost any malfunction. So it is with the Body of Christ; when one member hurts he ought to alert the other members to his need so they can move to meet it.

Since it is normally impractical for the entire church to respond in this way, the elders come in response to an ailing member's call. They, representing the church, will come and anoint him with oil and pray. The oil, in this case, is not medicinal, but symbolic. (Note that they *anoint*, not rub with oil.) Oil almost always symbolizes the ministry of the Holy Spirit, without whose restoration powers no one would ever be healed. The prayer of those believing men, based as it is on their full confidence on the Holy Spirit's capacity to heal, will restore the man both physically and spiritually.

Do you understand now what James is advocating? Essentially he is describing two approaches to this issue: (1) Confession of sin to one another and intercession by supporting members of the Body will deliver us from sin and its damaging side effects. That is the principle enunciated in James 5:16. (2) If, however, sin has run its course and in the process ravaged our bodies, even then we can call the elders of the local Body with which we are associated. If our sickness is the direct result of sin, then the prayer of the believing elders will result in both spiritual and physical restoration. That, it seems to me, is clearly James' conclusion in 5:14, 15.

From James' treatment of this theme, then, we can draw a rather startling conclusion. An open, caring, sharing community ought to be a more healthy community! Certainly that ought to be true in a spiritual sense. I believe that it is also true in a physical sense. Christians, to be sure, have their share of sickness and inevitably all die. Certainly no one is immune to the overall effects of sin in the world and in our bodies. James himself makes that clear in his book. Christians do suffer and die. However, in general, we ought to expect a greater measure of physical well-being in those groups where men and women are realistic and candid about their inner lives and where there is a mutual sharing and bearing of one another's sins. Certainly the physical well-being of the Sons of Israel was conditioned by their obedience (Deut. 7:15; 28:59, 61). It appears from this passage in James, moreover, that the principle is an enduring one. Therefore, keep on confessing your sins to one another that you may be healed.

THE FINAL WORD

This is James' last word, and it's a good one—one worth heeding. It has always struck me that James has no real conclusion to his epistle, at least not a formal salutation or conclusion. It ends very abruptly—no benediction, doxology, or farewell word. Perhaps it is because he does not want to deflect his readers' minds from these last thoughts. They seem to hang in the air and then reverberate in our memories.

> My brethren, if any among you strays from the truth, and one turns him back; let him know that he who turns a sinner from the error of his way will save his soul from death, and will cover a multitude of sins (James 5:19, 20).

Sad to say, some will stray from the truth. Perhaps it will be one of us! I certainly know the feeling. As the hymn writer puts it, "Prone to wander, Lord I feel it. Prone to leave the God I love." We are all susceptible to spiritual wanderlust. But what do we do when one among us strays? Well, James declares, rescue him, turn him around, turn him back. Get him headed for home. That's the counterpart to the discussion in 5:14–18. There the brother recognizes his need, and we come to his rescue. But what if he does not know or admit his need. He's lost and doesn't know it or doesn't want to be found. What do we do then? We seek and find him and turn him back. As Paul writes in Galatians 6:1, 2:

> Brethren, even if a man is caught in any trespass, you who are spiritual, restore such a one in a spirit of gentleness; looking

to yourself, lest you too be tempted. Bear one another's burdens, and thus fulfill the law of Christ.

That is love in action—the fulfillment of the law of love.
    You have undoubtedly heard the story of the boy who
was trudging through the ghetto with a small crippled
child on his back. When asked how he could carry such a
heavy load, he responded, "He ain't heavy. He's my
brother!" When you see a straying saint, he's your
brother—therefore he ain't too heavy. Pick him up and
help him along. James says that in so doing we will turn
a sinner from the error of his way, we will save his soul
from death, and we will cover a multitude of sins. By "saving a soul from death," James may have in mind the sin
unto death of which he speaks in 5:14–15. In that case he
would be using *soul* interchangeably with *person*. That may
well be. It seems more likely, however, that James is thinking metaphorically, and referring not to physical death, but
to that deathlike state of soul that settles in when we try
to evade the truth. We have all experienced this death—the
boredom, frustration, and emptiness which is the consequence of disobedience. When we turn a brother away
from his rebellion, we save a brother from such a condition.
    Furthermore, James states, we will "cover a multitude
of sins." That's a quotation from Proverbs 10:12: "Hatred
stirs up strife, But love covers all transgressions." The po-
etic parallelism here indicates that this action is antithetical
to "stirring up strife." Love takes a different tack. It covers
up sins. It doesn't harp on them (cp. Prov. 11:13). The stress
is on conciliation and peacemaking. Love doesn't make
trouble for a sinner. It makes peace. It is restorative and
redemptive. It hushes up the matter. It covers the sins with
love and points the way back home. That is a high and holy
calling. That is working the works of God.
    And who of us is adequate for those things—any of those

things we have read in the Book of James? What will keep us from "straying from the truth" as James puts it? James has stressed throughout his little epistle that the truth is *something to be done.* For him truth was not merely a matter of study, research, or discussion. It was something to which he submitted his entire humanity. God's truth is an affair of the heart and the hands. It is something by which James lived. He wholeheartedly endorsed it and lived it, and thus was liberated by it.

Freedom is not the liberty to do as we please. That so-called freedom shortly becomes tyranny of the worst sort (Gal. 5:13–15). True freedom—the only freedom worthy of the name—is the result of obedience to the will and character of God. As the Lord put it, "you shall know [in experience] the truth, and the truth shall make you free" (John 8:32). By faith we *can* work the works of God (James 2:23). By dependence on the indwelling life of our risen Lord, we *can* live lives free from bitter jealousy, selfish ambition, prejudice, and pride. Our tongues *can* be harnessed for redemptive and constructive purposes. We *can* be peaceable, gentle, reasonable people, stable and poised in the face of adversity and stress.

That's what makes life exciting. That makes it all worthwhile. And again, how do you do it? How do you become authentically Christian? It is by faith that you work the works of God. God alone is your adequacy and strength. Authentic faith works! All other belief is dead, demonic and downright dull.